Praise for
My Kid's an Honor Student, Your Kid's a Loser

"This is a great combination of hilarity and common sense . . . Ralph Schoenstein is not only funny, he's right!"

—Betty Rollin,
author *First, You Cry* and *Last Wish*

"A genuinely witty book. Parents have got to read it, not just for all its great humor but all its great wisdom, too."

—Peter Benchley

"Hilarious, a sagacious, side-splitting social commentary written by a great humorist whose wit and wisdom have had me laughing for some thirty years."

—W. C. Heinz

"Ralph Schoenstein writes these marvelous smiling pages, with each one prompting glee from the reader. And then you happen to notice that underneath all laughs there are these ferocious teeth. You notice because the teeth bite through the laughter. I don't know anybody except Schoenstein who can do this. It is the writer's art at its gaudiest."

—Jimmy Breslin

"Schoenstein brings humor and personal experience . . . this book will appeal to parents, both the driven and the more relaxed."

–*Booklist*

"Irreverent, funny."

–*Newark Star-Ledger*

"A fun and wise volume."

–*Chattanooga Times*

MY KID'S AN HONOR STUDENT, YOUR KID'S A LOSER

Also by Ralph Schoenstein

MY KID'S
AN HONOR STUDENT,
YOUR KID'S A LOSER

THE PUSHY PARENT'S GUIDE
TO RAISING THE PERFECT CHILD

Ralph Schoenstein

PERSEUS
PUBLISHING
A Member of the Perseus Books Group

Many of the designations used by manufacturers and sellers to distinguish their products are claimed as trademarks. Where those designations appear in this book, and where Perseus Publishing was aware of a trademark claim, the designations have been printed in initial capital letters.

Library of Congress Control Number: 2003101193
ISBN 0–7382–0851–5

Perseus Publishing is a member of the Perseus Books Group.
Find us on the World Wide Web at http://www.perseuspublishing.com.

Perseus Publishing books are available at special discounts for bulk purchases in the U.S. by corporations, institutions, and other organizations. For more information, please contact the Special Markets Department at the Perseus Books Group, 11 Cambridge Center, Cambridge, MA 02142, or call (800) 255–1514 or (617) 252–5298, or e-mail j.mccrary@perseusbooks.com.

Text design by Reginald Thompson
Set in 12-point Goudy

First paperback printing, March 2003

1 2 3 4 5 6 7 8 9 10—06 05 04 03

For Jill and Loren
My Favorite Parents
With Love

Contents

A birdie with a yellow bill
Hopped upon the windowsill,
Cocked his shining eye and said,
"Admissions just sent word: You're dead."

A Child's Garden of Reverses

Representing his two year-old daughter, a talent agent named Newt began to boil when the preschool director said, "I'm putting Katie in the lower twos."

"The lower twos?" cried Newt, ready to announce a deal breaker. "She's smart enough for the upper twos!"

"The class division is not by intelligence," the director said, wondering about Newt's "It's by age."

Silently, Newt wondered about a recount for his daughter's age.

Prelude: Good Morning, Madness

Every weekday morning at eight o'clock, just before leaving for the kindergarten of a Princeton, New Jersey, public school, six-year-old Roger Stark recites the Gettysburg Address for his father, Sam, who winces if his little Lincoln again happens to say "dedicated to the preposition" or "We here highly dissolve." Roger has been dedicating a Civil War cemetery with his Cheerios every morning since the school term began. Sam feels it is altogether fitting and proper that Roger do this, not because he will be Lincoln in a school play, not because he suffers from a kind of oratorical OCD, and not because he is preparing for *Jeopardy!* Sam is trying to get the boy off the road to an embarrassing college, one whose name ten years from now Sam would not be able to drop but would have to conceal with soft indirection:

> Hey, Sam, where's Roger at school?
> Oh . . . he's around the Eastern seaboard.

Ivy League?
Almost. He'd like to be president, so we decided on
D.C.
Georgetown?
I'll get back to you on that; gotta run to a
colonoscopy now.

A CPA of fifty-three, Sam Stark would rather see his son
in traction than in a division three school. He wants the
boy's mind to be as well trained as his bladder has been so
that Harvard will want him, perhaps by the time he is
twelve. Sam knows that much of Roger's competition is a
new Korean War: Somewhere over her oatmeal, a six-year-
old named Kim is reciting Washington's Farewell to His
Troops.

By saying the Gettysburg Address day after day, Roger
not only has disciplined his mind, but he also has developed an empathy for John Wilkes Booth. Sam does not
mind this feeling because he wants Roger to know all about
Booth ("No, he *didn't* cry 'Semper *fidelis!*'") in preparation
for the PSATs. Simply getting A's in every subject is no
longer good enough.

"A" means Asians now, Sam thinks. The grade belongs
to them, so the boy needs every edge he can get. He does
already know so much, like all the state capitals, all the
presidents, and the twelve cranial nerves. I wonder if any
Japanese kids have found more than twelve. I wonder if
any Chinese kids know more than forty-three presidents or
the Latin version of "The Wheels on the Bus."

Sam has told Roger's kindergarten teacher to make the boy recite the Gettysburg Address as often as possible; and the teacher, not the brightest light in the scholastic firmament, has done so. Working together, Sam and the teacher have succeeded in turning Roger into a stutterer.

We can use that, Sam thinks. I'll make sure he knows that Demosthenes stuttered too, and he can mention that in his interviews, either smoothly or in spurts. I wonder if he can learn to say "Demosthenes" in less than a minute?

In his unbridled desire to launch Roger toward Cambridge, Sam is hardly a lone loony in America today. In fact, aware of the mental condition of hundreds of thousands of people like him, Harvard issued a paper called "Time Out or Burn Out for the Next Generation," which told of overwrought kids being driven to make elite elementary schools with admission rates lower than Harvard's, kids overbooked with activities to dazzle admissions officers, some of whom now wish they were working as baggage handlers instead.

Even before the Harvard paper came out, the Carnegie Corporation had released a report about an alarming new person called "the driven child." Today, this child is driven in every possible way as he studies flash cards while riding from soccer to French in the van of a woman talking on a cell phone to her pediatrician:

"I'm frankly worried about Rhonda's neurons. Is there any way to see if she has *enough?*"

Carnegie talked of the possible damage to very young brains by overstimulation. Even dormant older brains can see that America is now crawling with parents who are driving their darlings toward acceptances at both Harvard and the Menninger Clinic, parents who will sacrifice anything to make their children superior. They will even sacrifice the children.

The nation is crawling with parents who are crawling themselves. A few blocks from Sam and his wee Emancipator, Alice Grady, mother of nineteen-month-old Amanda, has been doing the educational crawl with Amanda from one Learning Zone to another. The Better Baby Institute has told Alice that Amanda can be more than just a normal happy child if the two of them do bonded crawling through what it calls Activity Centers. In them, Amanda can become a little human almanac by receiving the kind of daily drilling that produced confessions in North Vietnam.

Alice and Amanda are crawling past things on which are taped white cards with bold printing—**TABLE, CHAIR, DOOR, LAMP**—as if they are items at an auction for imbeciles. At the Learning Zone near **COUCH,** the crawlers stop and Alice picks up a pack of flash cards while thinking, I wish I knew: Does Yale prefer you to be deeper in elephants or fish? Oh, stop worrying, Alice; she'll make Yale when she makes Stuart Country Day and the dominoes start falling on the old fast track. Of course, if she *doesn't* make Stuart, it's all over for her; it's a shift at Wal–Mart. I would go to bed with the head of admissions at Stuart, but it's a woman.

"Okay, darling," says Alice, holding up two flash cards, "I want you to focus your intellect now and tell Mommy as fast as you can: Which one is the *tiger?*"

After a thoughtful suck of her thumb, Amanda points to the card that has a picture of a kangaroo and brightly says, "Tiger!"

Alice's heart sinks as she suddenly sees Amanda at New Mexico State with people who will be beauticians because they had lost their way in the jungle.

"No, precious, goddamn it, listen *up: this* is the tiger. It comes from Africa. There are no kangaroos in Africa."

There are no tigers in Africa either, but Alice was a C-plus at Dartmouth, where she dated too many Dekes. With clenched teeth, she now grabs another set of flash cards while Amanda uses one cute little finger to explore the inside of her nose.

"No, sweetheart, you mustn't do *that* at the interview or the very nice school won't pick *you.* It won't be enough just to stay dry. Now what letter is *this?*"

"Tiger!" says Amanda.

It's Leo's goddamn genes, Alice thinks; Amanda needs something to make up for them. We'll have to put her in fencing as well as Russian, ceramics, and violin. I wonder how many other kids are already on learner steroids. I wonder if Stuart has a urine test or just the IQ, EQ, and DNA?

Smiling desperately, Alice now crawls toward the Activity Center called Map Station, which is on the way to the Japanese Station. There she lifts Amanda up to a large wall map and says, "Now tell me: Where is Germany?"

Amanda points to Austria and Alice cries, "Yes! *That's* a kind of Germany!"

With an orgasm of pride, Alice now has a shining vision: This wondrous child will be knowing how a sperm swims by the time she is three!

Elatedly, Alice lowers Amanda, grabs a flash card in each hand, and says, "Now tell me instantly, sweetheart: Which would you rather see? A Picasso or a dog?" When Amanda points to the basset hound, Alice crashes to earth. Suddenly she understands the heartbreak of King Lear.

Not far from the wind-up Lincoln and the enriching obstacle course, a woman of twenty-six named Janet Kramer is wearing a $300 vibrating belt with two speakers in a pouch strapped to her bulging abdomen. By transmitting complex patterns of heartbeatlike sounds, the belt is designed to elevate the IQ of a fetus that Janet already knows is tops in its trimester. However, in spite of her deep pride in this quasi-child, Janet is now in her seventh month and worries that she has waited too long to start tummy tutoring. How many rival fetuses have learned things in their *second* trimester?

They could be learning the breast stroke, she thinks, and spatial relations, too. Okay, I can handle it. The *most* that Rachel could be behind is three months, and we can make those up postpartum, where a lot of learning is still done. Of course, I hope it's *Roy* and not *Rachel;* boys have no attention span, so the competition is weaker. A little Ritalin, a few tutors, and he's in Harvard Yard. And maybe a letter from a cardinal or two to lock it up. Thank God we're not in New York: 3,000 applications for 48 openings at Hunter. In New York, I'd have to use the Pope.

Not far from Janet, a woman of thirty-three named Beth, whose son Kevin is two years and three months, has propped him up again at an iMac in which a CD-ROM called *Jump-Start Kindergarten* has just begun to flash quizzes that involve words, numbers, and shapes. Kevin gets every answer right because this is his twenty-ninth journey through *Jump-Start Kindergarten*—a chimpanzee would score well, too. Nevertheless, Beth knows he is ready for the Gettysburg Address or even the Cooper Union speech.

When Kevin reaches kindergarten three years from now, Beth will be giving him *Jump-Start Fifth Grade*, for she plans to continuously have him between five and ten years ahead of where his school thinks he is. She is certain that his mind is good enough to stand this schizophrenia and to fake current learning while simultaneously leaping ahead. When Kevin enters the Ivy League college of his choice, he will be doing *Jump-Start Medical School*, and when he enters medical school, he will be doing *Jump-Start Cosmetic Surgery*.

"It's the maddest thing going on, this obsession by young parents to create geniuses," says Dr. Benjamin K. Silverman, coauthor of *Pediatric Emergency Medicine*, a book in which this phenomenon belongs. "It has changed the whole nature of child rearing. I know one mother of an eighteen-month-old who already has talked to the admissions director of Yale."

What does the mother of an eighteen-month-old say to the admissions director of Yale? Perhaps:

> It might be helpful for you to know that Lisa's
> mobile contains a scene from the Sistine Ceiling,
> she never plays with toys just for fun, and she is
> working with a consultant to develop her eye con-
> tact because she seems interested in neurosurgery.
> She is in the upper 99th percentile of her sandbox.

Of course, not *all* parents are trying to launch their toddlers toward Yale: There is also what Alfie Kohn, a Boston
writer on education, calls "Preparation H—the big push to
get kids into Harvard. Parents are not raising a child. They
are raising a living résumé."

MY KID'S
AN HONOR STUDENT,
YOUR KID'S A LOSER

1

By the Authority Vested in You

"What's *your* résumé?" you are saying.

I'm not crazy about your tone, but I respect your question. Before you explore the scary new world of push-parenting with me, you might want to know, as my wife often does, if I have any idea what I'm talking about.

My only degree is a B.A.; but I did postgraduate work with the federal government and I am a corporal, United States Army, retired. I have three grown daughters, one grown wife, and two grandchildren. For forty years I have been a freelance writer, a calling that does not always inspire the deepest respect. About twenty years ago a friend of my wife's asked her, "Is Ralph working yet, or is he still writing?"

However, for four decades I have worked at something of cosmic importance: fathering and grandfathering, and I am now the same kind of authority on parenting that you are. *Everyone* is an authority on parenting and *no one* is. If you can understand this paradox, you can understand why you can get little help from a book when one of your children has just been attacked by a sibling who suddenly wants to be an only child; or when your child tells you that the prime rib you have just served her is yucky; or when you leave for a vacation and your child asks as you pull out of the driveway, "Are we there yet?"

Expertise on parenting is as useful as a pamphlet that might be called *What to Do When Attacked by a Shark*.

> First, if you happen to be afraid, don't let the shark know. With either a small hammer or your fist, punch the shark smartly on the snout, being careful to let him know that you are making a reasoned response and not an unprovoked assault.

Written expertise on parenting is as all wet as that pamphlet would have been if you could have found a few seconds to read it. In parenting, as Dr. Spock used to say, you can always trust your instincts, even if one of them is to put the child into the space program. Raising a child has always been a blend of groping, hoping, love, and luck, not necessarily in that order. Columnist Richard Cohen, who knows as much and as little as the rest of us, nicely sums it all up by saying, "Anyone can raise a kid, and over the course of history, just about everyone has. Almost always, the kid turns out okay."

Even Old Mother Hubbard's kids, who were raised on a diet in a 13E, probably turned out all right, although they were thin and didn't do much for Mother's Day.

Throughout the sixties and seventies, my wife Judy, a teacher, and I raised our first two daughters using no books but Dr. Spock and Dr. Seuss. Because the girls were almost four years apart, they were able to be friends when they weren't fighting; and because I waited in vain for maturity to come to me, I often felt like a contemporary when I played with them. I had no choice but to stay in touch with my inner child, because my inner child was a bossy kid, one who had moved my first daughter at the age of four to say, "Daddy, what will you be when you grow up?"

You had better know now that your guide in this book is a man who has sometimes broken into singing "Zippity-dee-doo-dah" on the street, an audition for the funny farm; a man who used to tap his small daughter on the shoulder, cry "Got you last!" and then sprint away, a sport less recommended than golf by the AARP.

In those happy years of singing and sprinting, I held tightly to parenting, because it distracted me from the frequent awareness that I was alone in a random and indifferent universe, a thought that can spoil your whole day. My best response to this thought was to think of a bedtime song I had written and sung to my youngest daughter whenever, in her earliest years, she had told me she was afraid:

> Now run along home
> And jump into bed.
> Close your eyes
> And unscrew your head.

No matter how loose my head might have been, my parenting was passionate and full time, though it did have a certain latitude, one the length of Canada.

"You never say no to the girls," Judy told me one night while one of them was breaking in new shoes by jumping on my abdomen.

"Of *course* I do," I said, then turned to tell my descending darling, "No, not *there*. . . . Oh, that's all right, honey. Now let's see if you know how to spell 'hernia.'"

"Your permissiveness makes Mister Rogers look like Torquemada," Judy said.

"But turning me into a trampoline is something the two of us do *together*," I said.

Judy did, of course, have a point: I was quite selective about the no's I said to the girls—for example, no getting tattooed and no eloping on school nights. I was a natural for the role of good cop, so the girls at times got mixed messages; but they were never uncertain about what to do: *Ask Dad*.

Parenting for Judy and me, an endlessly improvised stumbling along, was both the noblest profession and the sweetest way of life. However, when the girls were fifteen and eleven, Judy wistfully said to me one day, "They're growing up so fast. Do you realize that soon we'll be able to start doing things just by ourselves?"

"You want a life of your *own?*" I replied. "That's pretty self-indulgent, I'd say."

I was coming down with the first known case of premature empty-nest syndrome. I was imagining the sadness I would feel when the girls were grown up, something I had forbidden them to do.

And then, one evening the following year, Judy dropped into my lap and said, "I have something I think you should know. I'm pregnant."

"That's *wonderful!*" I cried.

"Well . . . yes, of course. But in case you haven't noticed, we've already *got* two. And I'm not twenty-one—or *thirty*-one."

"Honey, just tell me this: Has anything else ever been more fun for us than the kids?"

"I wouldn't know," she said. "We've never *tried* anything else."

And so, this is the man who will be your guide as we drop down the rabbit hole of the résumé raisers and into a world where parents are competing to see whose child can be pushed out of childhood first, a world that moved one cartoonist to show a mother asking a father, "But if everyone's children achieve, how will we know ours are superior?"

These people drive a car with a bumper sticker that tastefully announces their pride:

MY KID'S AN HONOR STUDENT
YOUR KID'S A LOSER

We are about to explore the shrinking of both American childhood and American brains in a land where a Web site called SmarterKids.com lets parents plumb their toddlers' linguistic, cognitive, and social-emotional skills.

What, you wonder, is a social-emotional skill for a one-year-old? Not wetting the rug of the Harvard Club? Not swallowing a place card? Not spitting up at the opera?

Perhaps the child must mature for a year, like the two-year-old whose father proudly told SmarterKids.com that she could give her full name, point to six body parts, and use contractions. In short, this daughter of the brave new America could say, "I am Lucy Ann Hammerschlagg, and this, this, this, this, this, and this isn't my spleen."

Or should she have said "*aren't* my spleen"?

Somewhere right now, a child is crawling toward a laptop to make a grammar check. And his mother is clocking his time.

2

A Lombardi Lullaby

I begin my odyssey with a confession: As a father of three and a grandfather of two, I not only have seen the new lunacy growing, I have been a part-time lunatic myself, sometimes on the fringe and sometimes at the fearsome core. My only excuse is that, like Sam, Alice, and Janet, I have lived in a country full of ostensible adults who are possessed by a lust to be Number One, people whose passion is to keep giving the world the second finger and sometimes the third. American competitiveness is so fierce that, in the dreary spirit of that bumper sticker, flaunting your own supremacy isn't enough: You must also make a heartfelt statement that everyone else sucks. Some historian undoubtedly will soon discover that both Genghis Khan and Attila the Hun were Americans.

I was drawn into the great parenting Olympics when my first daughter was born and I went to the glass window of the hospital nursery to stand beside the enemy, the people who poignantly had come to admire their inferior infants. To objective eyes, however, my daughter's superiority to all the nondescript babies beside her still would have been instantly clear. Elbowing away a rival father, I gazed at my daughter in awe, noticing that she had been born with remarkably long eyelashes. And then I turned to that father and said, "Would you like to see something?"

Piteously, he was under the impression that he was seeing something already.

"Look at the *eyelashes* on *this* one," I said, pointing to the room's outstanding infant.

"Yes, how about that?" he weakly said.

"They look like little Japanese fans," I said, implying that *his* child had venetian blinds.

These words snapped him out of his pointless reverie and into a counterattack.

"*That* one is *mine*," he said, pointing to a routine child. "Just look at his *fingers*."

"More than ten?" I said, and we both laughed insincerely.

"Well," he said, "the important thing is health."

"Absolutely. What's your baby's pulse?"

Forty years later, that paternal combat at the nursery window seemed like warm camaraderie when I went to adore my granddaughter at another nursery window, where again I stood surrounded by misinformed Magi. In those forty years, most American parents had decided that life was worth living only if you were living it through a gold medal child. You couldn't flaunt a silver, and a bronze would reduce you to pitiable hugs in dark rooms.

Gazing now at my first granddaughter, I was happy to see that she unquestionably was the prettiest child in the nursery, and perhaps in the Northern Hemisphere. I felt sorry for all the other babies in the nursery, because they would need good personalities. My granddaughter's personality, of course, also seemed to be splendid. I had needed just seconds to know that she had both the face of a Madonna and the heart of Mother Teresa, exceptional traits for a Jewish child.

Turning to another new grandfather, I said, "Is yours a boy or a girl?" I had to find something about the baby that rated a comment, so I graciously pretended to be interested in the baby's gender. The man's answer would have involved me only if he had said, "Neither."

"A *boy*," he said with misplaced pride. "*That* one. He's as cute as he can be!"

"Yes, I know that limit," I said, "and he *has* come quite close to it." And then I pointed to the nursery's masterpiece. "Mine is *this* one with the incredibly long eyelashes."

I didn't like repeating myself with lash flaunting, but I gambled that he hadn't been around for the birth of this baby's mother.

At once he struck back with the ferocity that was now inflaming the parents of the American Superkid.

"Our baby's Apgar scores are 9.8," he said.

It was a sneak attack, telling me that the kid had a 9.8 Apgar. Momentarily off balance, I wondered what the record was. I didn't know what an Apgar was, so I didn't know whether to go higher or lower in trying to trump him. Would a 10 have been better? Or, in this new Olympics, would a *better* Apgar time have been a 9.6?

"Apgar?" I casually said. "Is that his sugar count?"

"No, it's the SAT for infants: tests for breathing, muscle tone, heart rate, reflexes, and color. Your granddaughter may have been absent when it was given."

"No," I said, now determined to make him feel as lousy as I could, "she'll be taking her Apgar with the next class. But she *is* already in the 95th percentile for height and weight. Does your boy happen to be in a percentile?"

"He doesn't want to peak too soon."

Three weeks later, I was thrown into battle again. Not wanting to be belligerent, I revealed my sensitivity when I said to a passing grandmother, "You know, my granddaughter Laura is just three weeks old and she's already starting to watch a mobile of birds over her crib."

"That's remarkable," she said with an icy smile, "because Spock says that mobile watching never starts before one month."

"Spock had a criminal record," I said. "Not that he didn't know pediatrics, of course."

"This is my grandson Brandon," she said, producing a picture with the speed of a Dodge City gunfighter.

"Yes, I'm sure it is. Yes, look at that. He's definitely a grandson."

"He's already toilet trained. He knows that the toilet is his friend."

"And he'll need all he can get. You might enjoy knowing that Laura makes the cutest faces when she moves her bowels. I'm sorry I can't show you a picture."

"They all look cute when they do that, even the homely ones. By the way, tell your daughter not to expect Laura to be toilet trained as early as Brandon. Few children have that kind of talent."

"Really? Then the money you save on diapers you can use for therapy. A new study says that it may be better not to be toilet trained at *all*. It's an alternate lifestyle now, and possibly a risky one for mental health. Of course, the work done with Brandon *is* impressive, even if it leads to problems at the other end."

Now that millions of parents have shut down their own lives to live entirely through their children, the competition can chill the blood, whose hemoglobin count can reach 19 in overachievers. The moment a parent sees a child she didn't happen to deliver, she must ask herself: What can that child do and how can I top it, disparage it, or disprove it?

My own guard should have been higher in an encounter I had when my second daughter, Lynn, was ten months old. Not only was she able to walk at that age but she also could go through a book called *Pat the Bunny* and produce the proper responses to every page. In fact, my wife and I sometimes took Lynn and her favorite literature to the homes of people we wanted to stop seeing.

"Lynn is certifiably beyond belief," I casually said one day to the mother of a child who also happened to be ten months old. "She was able to do every single thing in *Pat the Bunny* at eight months. She'll probably major in either literature or small animals at Wellesley."

The woman paused for a moment to absorb the blow and then she said, "You know, they're doing wonderful work these days with young gorillas. I hear that some of them have even learned how to rub the bunny's fur. My own daughter happens to prefer outdoor sports to literature. She's not yet a year and she already knows how to swim."

That exchange took place in 1970. Today, a ten-month-old swimmer would hardly score against an enemy parent. Instead, the mother would have to say, "She's going to learn how to swim the moment she gets tired of walking on the water."

3

Fetal Academy

If, as both Sartre and Herbert Hoover have said, life is absurd, then no embracing of the absurdity is warmer than the pregnant young women who are turning their wombs into classrooms, the mothers who are trying to improve the partial minds of their potential children. These women have transcended the question: When does life begin? to ask: When does *homework* begin and how can my clearly extraordinary semichild get that vital first jump on all his fetal foes? How can he hit the placenta running on the fast track to the Ivy League? How can I avoid wasting the gestation so it won't merely be nine months off for him? It is absolutely tragic to see mothers whose babies are curriculum-free.

When my wife, Judy, was pregnant with each of our three daughters, she did no utero tutoring because she was too simple to realize that the trimesters were semesters in prepartum prep, that they were a soggy private school.

Foolishly presuming that fetuses were incommunicado, Judy had set her sights so low that all she kept yearning for were healthy babies.

Many years later, I looked around America to see if American attempts to communicate with life in outer space had been pushed aside by attempts to communicate with life in inner space—a greater challenge, because we hadn't been trying to make the aliens smarter. Of course, they may already have been smart enough to know to let sleeping fetuses lie.

I began by tuning in to a Ph.D. named Carista Luminare-Rosen, codirector of the Center for Creative Parenting in Marin County, the place in America with a grip on reality as tight as that of the Wizard of Oz. Calling herself a pre-natal counselor, which sounded like someone who taught volleyball at a camp for embryos, Luminare-Rosen said that there were specific ways to communicate with a child in the womb: by playing music, by talking out loud to the child, and by writing letters to the child.

I had heard about the supposedly beneficial use of music, but I wondered about language: How could a fetus with even excellent hearing, one who could hear underwater, make sense of his mother saying, "Darling, remember for the Dalton interview that the square root of nine is three, the Caspian Sea is a lake, and the capital of Libya is Tripoli"? And I also wondered how mail could be sent to someone who was in the kind of position that Houdini liked to assume. It seemed to me that for a fetus there could be only one kind of delivery.

It also seemed so to the *Lancet*, the British medical journal, which told of a study revealing that the most a fetus could learn was how to recognize a repeated sound for about ten minutes, precisely the attention span of many students in classes outside the womb. In this British study, the fetus received a stimulation of both vibration and sound just above its legs. Ten minutes later, it received the double stimulation again and stopped moving, showing that it remembered the sounds, was bored by them, and had stopped paying attention. This was training for attention deficit disorder (ADD), not MIT, although it might have been possible for a mother to reverse the experiment, try to keep the fetus in action, and go for an athletic scholarship. To the creator of a Superbaby, an athletic scholarship makes sense if the fetus hasn't revealed Ivy League intelligence, if he still doesn't know all the chemical elements and state capitals.

"Parents interested in prenatal communication have taught their prenates the 'Kick Game,'" says Dr. David B. Chamberlain, editor of *Prenatal Memory and Learning.* "When the babies kick, the parents touch the abdomen and say, 'Kick, baby, kick!' And then, after the baby has kicked again, they move to a different location and repeat the invitation. Babies soon oblige by kicking anywhere on cue."

The promise of this experiment is so intoxicating that it makes one think: One small kick for mankind, one giant kick for man. If babies *are* able to master a fourth-down play, then the next step is teaching them to pass, or at least to fall on the ball. However, it seems that a fetus in this first lower school is able to major only in phys. ed. because there have to be limits to what his little half-head can do.

In another British study, fetuses were exposed to the repeated singing of tunes and the best they could do was eventually remember them and stop responding. Here was a dramatic demonstration of how to bore children. Parents, however, have always known how, especially at dinner.

"Anyway, what do the *British* know?" the fast-track American mother might say. "They call private schools *public* schools and they don't even let the parents visit. They put education entirely in the hands of *teachers*, which explains why they lost all their colonies, even Bermuda."

The British view that fetuses are basically learning disabled is shared by Dr. John Cotton, a Princeton pediatrician, who says, "Teaching your baby in the womb is just absurd; there is *no* scientific basis for it. But that doesn't stop a lot of marketing that sells to these people."

It is a bull market in bullshit for babies, and it will survive any recession because the fetal follies and the drive for postnatal perfection are forces of nature in America now. Older, wealthier, and better educated than their own parents had been, new parents are giving their children what they themselves never got: a loving shove in the wrong direction.

Even though there have been almost no medical studies on the prenatal reading of mail, playing the saxophone, or any other kind of learning, a fast-track mother still might point to one study at the University of North Carolina.

Sixteen women read *The Cat in the Hat* to their fetuses twice a day for the last six weeks of their pregnancies. When the babies were born, *The Cat in the Hat* was read to them again and they supposedly showed a preference for it by sucking faster. However, babies who hadn't heard Seuss in the womb did postpartum sucking at the same constant rate, whether hearing Seuss or the Pledge of Allegiance. Fortunately for Sam and Roger, there has been no fetal training in the Gettysburg Address, although it is only a matter of time before some womb in Yokohama hears the Second Inaugural.

Once again we must ask: How could the professional mother use such learning to give her rare jewel the first admission in the row of scholastic dominoes? An admission to a domino is a flawed metaphor, but I did a lot of goofing off in the womb and I even took naps that should have gotten me detention. To answer the question: One thing this mother can do is teach her child to tell the interviewer:

> My name is Max, not Sam-I-am;
> Want to hear just how I cram?
> Well, I have known the ways of a Druid
> Since early days in my Mommy's fluid.

In spite of scientific discouragement from both sides of the Atlantic, the fast-track mother can still draw hope from people like a Seattle doctor named Brent Logan, who disagrees with all the evidence and says, "prenatal teaching can make a child physically, mentally, and socially mature, with an IQ of up to two hundred."

It is a vision to trigger awe, among other emotions: A girl of four at a dinner party, ignoring premenstrual tension to make a joke in Latin while selecting the right fork.

The fast-track mother's best hope for getting a jump on all her rivals may be not chanting but the tummy belt on Janet Kramer. The belt plays sixteen audiotapes that deliver sonic patterns to excite the fetal nervous system, exercise the fetal brain, and possibly damage both permanently. Obstetricians say that prenatals *are* made restless by sound, but they might be trying to get *away* from it, and intense sound might even do harm. The fetus might be learning to think, That stuff hurts where my ears will be. And even softer, it would still stink. Doesn't she have any Billy Joel?

The competitive mother, however, laughs at risk because she dares to drive her child to new heights, like those reached by the rats who were exposed in utero to a Mozart sonata at the University of Wisconsin in 1988. After birth, the rats that had studied Mozart were able to complete a maze more rapidly and with fewer errors than rats that had heard only Fats Waller.

This research cries out for further development. If Mozart can help rats get through a maze, then what could Haydn teach to hamsters that could get them into a Harvard lab? And Wagner for Dobermans dreaming of protecting Ph.D.'s?

Of course, no matter how quickly hamsters run, they are on a wheel that doesn't lead to the Ivy League. They are a species that doesn't need a CD called *The Mozart*, which has been a hit since 1988, when American parents began playing it for their own fetuses instead of playing Brahms's "Lullaby." At best, Brahms leads to deferred decisions. The intelligently pushy parent knows which Mozart piece to send to the fetal cerebral cortex, for not just any Mozart will exalt the coming IQ. In addition to the music on *The Mozart*, the big four of fetal fast-forward are *Mozart for Babies' Minds* (Violin Concerto #3), *Mozart Playtime* (Minuet in F Major), *Parents Magazine Classical Music for Baby Mozart* (Serenade #13 in G Major), and *Mozart for Toddlers* (Symphony #35). If a mother is foolish enough to play something worthless, like the *Jupiter* symphony, she is taking a chance on getting a toe-tapping nitwit.

In his book *The Mozart Effect*, Don Campbell says that words can be as miraculous as music: "Read to your baby in the womb and have your partner do the same. Classics like *The Little Prince* are recommended. Make up songs with lyrics like 'Hello, baby, this is Dad. We'll be welcoming you soon.' Don't be self-conscious. It will be quite a few more years before your child has the capacity to be judgmental."

Campbell's last thought is beyond dispute: No matter what homework your fetus does in the womb, even if he takes gestation pass-fail, he is not likely to be critical, even of "Hello, baby, this is Dad. We'll be welcoming you soon," a lyric almost as elegant as "Who let the dogs out?"

The potential for inspiring early achievement boggles the mind; and boggling the mind, even when it resembles a pimiento, is now the sacred mission of many American parents with a mania to make their children perform intellectual feats even earlier than the children of the great Swiss psychologist Jean Piaget, whose kids were late bloomers compared to our world-class toddlers.

He may have lived near Salzburg, but Jean Piaget never knew about the Mozart Effect, an American discovery to take its place beside the Edsel, the New Coke, and the Reggie bar. I wonder what he would have said about all the Americans who now believe that hearing Mozart not only can produce a higher class of rats but can also raise their children's intelligence.

I do know what is said by Samuel Glucksberg, professor of psychology at Princeton, who told me, "The Mozart Effect has absolutely no validity and has been disproved in several studies, but the nonsense is so widespread that the governor of Georgia gave every newborn child a Mozart CD paid for by the state."

Are you still wondering why the South lost that war?

Parents wanting to get a jump even on those getting a jump on Piaget can go beyond Don Campbell's lyrics and Janet Kramer's belt to the work of an Ohio pioneer named Joseph Susedik, author of *A Spark of Genius—The World's First Prenatal Teaching Book,* who claims to have made all four of his children geniuses by speaking directly to his wife's stomach and presuming that the fetus would take the call.

"I visualized exactly where the baby was," Joseph Susedik told me, "and I talked to it."

A three-dimensional teaching program goes on between a pregnant porpoise and it's [sic] young in utero, is one thought from the book by Joseph Susedik, who didn't learn in or out of the womb the difference between a contraction and a possessive pronoun. *You must remember that the baby can be taught much more at a time prenatally because there is not much to distract it in the womb. Let the baby grasp a really good knowledge of our language before you start teaching with academics.*

Does teaching with academics mean you should have a professor beside you at your wife's belly? The answer already may have been found at pre–Ivy League schools with names like the Prelearning Institute, Prenatal University, and the Prenatal Institute, where fathers put their faces to gestating geniuses and say, "Hi, baby, this is *Daddy!*" Does the baby have caller ID? Possibly: A faculty member at one of the Prenatal Institutes says, "By the time the baby is born, it will know fifty useful words." Perhaps some will be these: "Hi, Daddy. Sorry I didn't get back to you; I was tied up. Should I go into therapy now or wait till I'm two?"

If Prenatal University had a team, its cheerleaders could use a pregaphone, the latest invention in broadcasting on a fetal frequency. A large plastic plunger attached to a smaller one by a hose, the pregaphone is particularly designed for parents whose voices are low. Nothing, however, has yet been invented to raise *their* IQs.

Today throughout the United States of Acceleration, teaching babies in the womb is being vigorously explored by parents seeking the ultimate head start. And this age of electronic marvels will surely reach a day when a sonogram will be a class picture for a mother whose navel will have a transmitter for her own PBS: Prenatal Broadcasting System.

"Good morning, class," she will say, delighted again by the student-teacher ratio. "I hope you remember everything we covered about the French Revolution; there'll be a quiz in the delivery room. Now, today we're going to cover the rise of Napoleon, who was not much bigger than you."

And someday in that delivery room, a mother will be speaking this prayer:

"Let her be born gifted, not abnormal. Let her be *more* gifted than all the ordinarily gifted kids. Let her somehow know that Pluto is no longer a planet, that Woodrow Wilson's first name was Thomas, and that 'Take the A Train' was written by Billy Strayhorn, not Duke Ellington. And let her know that childhood is a condition that I'll help her out of just as fast as I can."

4

And a Little Child Shall Bleed Them

At nine o'clock one Monday morning at the YWCA of Princeton, New Jersey, I attended a class of America's youngest students, the ones enrolled in a course called Creepy Crawlers. As a student at college, I had taken a CC because Contemporary Civilization was a required course. At the YWCA, this CC also was required, but as a prerequisite for Fun for Ones, whose credits then enabled a student to move on to Gymantics, which launched the student on a sixteen-year flight toward the university down the road.

The students in the YWCA's Creepy Crawlers seemed cheerfully relaxed, except perhaps for the two who were screaming; but at every school, certain students are unhappy to have morning classes. My own college roommate had flirted with consciousness until ten o'clock.

It was important for the mothers to be there because each of them had her eyes on the prize and her foot on the

23

accelerator. Each of them felt that the moment an American child is born, he cries out not just for milk but for enrichment, enhancement, and early enrollment at the first domino. And some of them might even have known about the *Newsweek* report of a study revealing that breast-fed babies had IQs approximately eight points higher than bottle-fed ones. At last, there was a happier meaning for the words "boob tube."

Suddenly, however, when I saw the students placed in a circle before the young female teacher, I was struck by the folly of rushing childhood instead of slowly savoring it and trying to make it last, the folly of trying to *aid* that cruel enemy Time. The poet Andrew Marvell had written of "time's wingèd chariot"; and since the moment that I had made the mistake of turning sixty, I had wondered why time could not have avoided that chariot and taken a trolley car instead.

"Row, row, row your boat, gently down the stream," the teacher was singing to the students now. "Merrily, merrily, merrily, merrily, life is but a dream." The students were squirming and those last five words had me squirming, too, as I thought of the philosopher who had said, "All is flux." How I wished he had said "All is flax" or "All should floss" or anything else to keep me from the painful awareness of how fleeting were the precious days of these students, the awareness of how every day I had been moving further from the sweet frozen frames of photos of my own three daughters, toward whom I had always felt like a kind of cockeyed contemporary.

The students were on their backs now while their mothers put them through calisthenics by moving their tiny arms and legs as if they were rag dolls. After the calisthenics, the teacher began an anatomy lesson by singing, "Head and nose and feet and toes," and another student began to cry. The mothers were lifting the dolls and moving their legs in a new exercise, but I was seeing myself crossing the campus of Hamilton College for a reunion last year and wondering, Where did it all go and what did it all mean? Had it all really happened or had it all been just a dream? My own springy legs had been moving well on this visit, but my spongy mind had gone back to Winter Carnival 1952, where my companion, Miss Cookie Flynn, was having another orange blossom while preparing to throw up on her luminous pink gown, while Nat King Cole sang, "They tried to tell us we're too young . . ."

Yes, in the last line of "Row, Row, Row Your Boat," these Creepy Crawlers were getting a philosophical insight that had come to me much later. The song "Push 'Em, Point 'Em," however, was less profound, as was "To Market, to Market." And then the mothers were bouncing the Crawlers to another song, dribbling them to the beat of "The Wheels on the Bus," while I tried not to think of the bittersweet words that my wife had said last week to our youngest daughter, Lori: "I'd love to raise you all over again."

Judy and I would have raised all three of our daughters again because parenting was an adventure that made climbing Everest seem like a trip down the driveway. During all the raising, I kept wanting to freeze the best moments while thinking, This is as good as it gets. This is the proof of God that Aquinas missed. This is even better than sex during Bach.

But we had *raised* the girls: We hadn't *launched* them from pads like this, a carpet where the mothers now were rolling their students back and forth, each mother enjoying the softness while looking for an edge. Nat King Cole's song was meaningless today: Too young could have meant only an embryo that was waiting for fetal registration. So far, the class had been all gymnastics; but that of course was the requirement for the graduate work of Fun for Ones.

And now the class became rock and roll: After the rolling, the students were rocked in little chairs, except for one young man, who was pushed around the rug in a wheelbarrow. Moments later, the students were put down on their backs and given plastic toys, a nice recreational break from the rigors of the curriculum, while the mothers sang some of the nursery's Top Forty.

These women *were* feeling the bliss of handling their babies, but did they need the structure of a class to feel it? Everything they were doing at this pre-preschool had been done in natural improvisation by mothers from the beginning of time. Eve might have put Cain and Abel on their backs in the garden and sung, "The itsy-bitsy serpent goes up the water spout . . . "

When the class was ending, I remembered the words of that outlaw Benjamin Spock, "Play is the work of babies," and I wondered if there was ever a baby who needed vocational school. With its dizzy belief that nothing on earth should be exempt from betterment, America was now a country capable of teaching a rooster how to crow in a class called Here Comes the Sun.

At this YWCA, the graduates of Creepy Crawlers who were able to stand moved up to Fun for Ones. A student was allowed a certain amount of crawling in Fun for Ones, and first-year crawling would have carried no stigma in Finland or Bolivia; but first-year crawling in America did not auger well for the student's chance to make a top nursery school for a catapult to a top kindergarten. The admissions committee at Hunter or Dalton would have cringed at a letter from the dean of Fun for Ones saying, *Matthew has stopped eating his socks and he no longer throws up to make a statement, but he is not always vertical.*

Like Creepy Crawlers, Fun for Ones also required no attention span and also allowed the student to take crying as an elective. To make the transition from Creepy Crawlers easier for the student still adjusting to lower academic life, Fun for Ones also began each class in a circle, with each student placed inside a hula hoop. In the class I saw, however, the circle held its design for just a few seconds, until one of the students, a chubby blond girl, started to cry and ran away. She ran well and the mother chasing her probably thought about a track scholarship at Bryn Mawr.

Another student now began to pound his mother with his tiny fists, but a boxing scholarship was probably not on the mother's mind. However, she must have found comfort in the sight of the blond escapee's mother carrying her screaming back to the circle, for few sights are more heartwarming to a fast-track mother than a competitor having a fit. While the boxer's mother subdued him, the blonde continued to scream in counterpoint to the teacher, who was merrily trying to hold the circle together by singing:

> Tick-tock, tick-tock,
> I'm a little cuckoo clock.
> Now I'm striking one o'clock.
> Cuckoo! Cuckoo!

The last cuckoo triggered another escape: a curly-haired boy broke out, ran toward a big plastic cube, almost made it, but went down hard. Most of these students were like tiny prisoners in Stalag 1, and I felt for them because the academic experience is not at its peak of gratification when you keep falling down trying to escape.

"Parents are raising the bar too high," Professor Glucksberg says, "and when the kids fail, both the parents and the kids are disappointed."

"Absolutely," says Dr. Cotton. "Moreover, until the age of about three or four, most children don't interact; it's all parallel play."

In Fun for Ones, however, the play was not yet parallel but, rather, solitary distraction and distress.

"You can tell when they're not interested," the teacher told me. "They go limp."

Perhaps some instinctive wisdom told these kids that the best thing was to play dead and hope they'd be taken for resuscitation to a place where no one was making them roll through plastic hoops as the initial move toward Yale.

In addition to the blond girl and the curly-haired boy, one of the other students also felt that the circle held nothing of interest for her and was now starting to crawl away, followed by her crawling mother. I thought of Alice Grady crawling rewardingly after her Amanda as directed by the Institutes for the Achievement of Human Potential, and I wondered if this mother knew that she may have been crawling in fruitless incorrectness: there was a properly educational way to do it that separated Man from the lobster.

"Row, row, row your boat," the teacher now sang, and then reminded everyone that "life is but a dream." And the dreams can be chilly ones. In a nearby town, one mother recently had spent the night in her car so that when the Cranbury Presbyterian Nursery School opened in the morning, she would be the first one to apply for one of the few openings. Might knowing the janitor have given her an edge?

Knowing Windows 98 would have been better, for computer literacy is required in this new world, where my own grandson said when he was four, "If you want me to do something, Ralph, just click on me." He had said this to me one morning in his nursery school, the same one where I had been with my daughter Lori twenty-two years before. I stood with him in that same classroom and reeled at the thought of the most dismaying words I knew, *This too shall pass*, and wished again that these words referred only to kidney stones.

After the Fun for One students were processed through the hula hoops and then rolled on the rug a bit, the required curriculum was over and the teacher called for free play, which was precisely what each mother would have done with the child at home for no tuition. At the end of a half hour of free play, the circle was reassembled, the dreamy students again were reminded of the dreamy nature of life, and then the teacher sang:

> *Good-bye, children,*
> *Good-bye, children,*
> *Good-bye, children,*
> *It's time to say good-bye.*

It seemed to me that childhood also was getting a tuneful farewell.

5

When Push Comes to Shove

Push-parenting didn't begin the day that Harvard received its first inquiry about a promising fetus. Alexander the Great's mother pushed him to be more than just Alexander the Above Average; and Mozart's father was a push-parent who took the four-year-old boy on play dates all over Europe. However, only in the late 1990s did push-parenting sweep America as one of the most popular mental illnesses. In these last few years I have listened again and again to fashionably disturbed parents play scenes that were missing only the Mock Turtle, scenes like these . . .

At 4:40 one Tuesday afternoon on the East Side of Manhattan, ten minutes before she has to pick up her six-year-old daughter at a bassoon lesson for a cab ride to a lesson in Serbo-Croatian, Margaret DuBoff, a forty-four year-old professional mother, gets a cell phone call from Susanna Krebs, a professional mother of thirty-eight.

"Maggie," says Susanna, "could Destiny play with Melanie from four to five tomorrow? I'm bringing in someone from the State Department to talk about the Middle East, and he does magic, too. Melanie is hopelessly behind on free trade."

Quickly punching her PalmPilot with her free hand, Margaret says, "Oh, Susanna—" and suddenly wonders if Destiny knows enough Stephen Foster. "Destiny has her Introduction to Puberty Class on Wednesdays at four."

"What's the age of puberty now?"

"Well, the *Times* just said it *hasn't* gone down, but I don't want to take any chances."

"Maggie, has Destiny started to . . . ?"

"I only wish! Wouldn't it be *wonderful* for her résumé to include a line in *The Guinness Book of World Records?* You know, it seems she's been a child for *ages and ages*; I mean, there's got to be some statue of limitations!"

"*Statute.*"

"You *see? That's* why I got those 2,000 flash cards for the dictionary. I want Destiny to know more words than her mother by the time she hits Yale."

"So she hasn't had her first period yet."

"No, her first period is still origami. But when it does happen, I'm going to surprise her with the cutest little kit from Pads 'Я' Us."

"Well, no matter *when* Melanie's hormones kick in, I wish she'd stop acting so childish. My God, she's almost *five.*"

"Susanna, why don't you pencil Destiny in for the third Thursday in March at five. Right now, it seems to be free and I feel a bit guilty about that, so I'd love to book it."

"Maggie, I think it's terrific that Destiny is a bassoonist who speaks Serbo-Croatian. She could play with a Bosnian big band."

"If they're not well rounded, they may as well forget the Ivy League and go to leg waxing school."

"Peter must be so proud."

"He isn't her father. But somewhere a test tube is very proud."

"Have you told Peter that her father was a DH?"

"There's a right time for those things."

As she rides to pick up Destiny, Margaret's mind drifts back to the sperm bank, where seven years ago she went to create someone with a better chance to get into Yale than a child by Peter would have had. Yes, Yale: *In vitro veritas*. To give the child the ideal edge, Margaret also would have used a surrogate for herself, but she knew no one with nine free months; it was a big favor to ask of a friend.

At the sperm bank Margaret had biblically given herself to the director and two lab assistants in a poignant effort to learn the genes she was getting. All three men said that she was one of the best they'd ever had, but none would reveal the IQ of the new father. Of course, Margaret knew it would have to top Peter's—she could have done that at a zoo—so she simply prayed that she had a Rhodes scholar and not someone on parole.

And now my dearest is in the great race to New Haven or Cambridge, Margaret thinks, and she's at least a length ahead at the far turn. If a mother doesn't use the new eugenics, she's condemning her child to a safety school like Albany State.

Margaret wonders if she should have gone even beyond traditional in vitro to the work at the University of Oregon that inserted superior genes into an egg.

Is that fascism? she wonders. Well, I'll bet Mussolini's kids got into the best schools.

When she picks up Destiny, Margaret is so moved by the child's development that she suddenly bursts into song: *Where is the little girl I carried?*

"If you sing that song again," says Destiny, "I'm moving to Brazil."

"And what's the chief export of Brazil?"

"*Duh. Bicycles.*"

"Sweetheart, if you're a smartass at the interviews, Daddy will disinherit you. Now, what is the chief export of Brazil?"

"Coffee. I'm sorry; I'm in a bad mood. I got ninety-nine on a test, but Marnie Cockburn got a hundred and laughed at me."

"Life isn't fair, darling. Who said that?"

"Teddy Kennedy."

"*No . . .*"

"Oh, the other one."

"And remember: Next year Marnie Cockburn will still be stuck in a public school, doomed to being average all her life, while *you'll* be at Dalton. What's the capital of Belize?"

"Belmopan, of course."

"And what did *Belize* used to be?"

"Mom, even kids in the 98*th* percentile know *that*. British Honduras, *duh*."

"If you say *duh* one more time, I'm going to take away your blusher."

"Will they ask something that easy at the Dalton interview?"

"I'm trying to find out. I've offered the admissions director some bearer bonds."

Margaret remembers when she told Destiny's principal about planning a transfer to the first grade at Dalton.

No offense, Margaret had said, *but Destiny has been in public school much too long and I just hope it won't be held against her. She's been registered at the preschool of Ethical Culture since birth, but nothing has opened. I was hoping the encephalitis epidemic might've given her a place last year, but no such luck.*

Harry Truman went to a public school, the principal said.

Name another, Margaret replied.

"Melanie's mother just called to schedule a play date," says Margaret to Destiny in the cab. "Check the third Thursday in March at five."

Destiny punches her PalmPilot and says, "Oh yes, I'm free. But don't you think I should do something proactive with the time? Maybe some power yoga."

"Yes, more power yoga can give you an edge."

"I mean, just playing doesn't *mean* anything, does it?" says Destiny.

"No, it certainly doesn't. And the other thing is . . . well, Melanie strikes me as being just a teensy bit—how can I put this?—*normal*—in the scholastic, not psychiatric sense, of course—and if you do have to play, you should keep playing *up*."

At dinner that evening, eaten quickly so that Destiny can make her seven o'clock ballet class, Margaret and Peter again make the kind of momentous conversation that Joseph P. Kennedy made at meals with his children.

"What do you think of Mexico devaluing the peso?" says Peter to Destiny.

"Cool," she says.

With a harsh look, Margaret says, "*Destiny*."

"Sorry; *frío*."

"That's better. The student tied to English is the one who attends *la escuela inferior*."

"But, dear, is Spanish the ideal language for admissions?" says Peter. "Drug lords speak it and Harvard knows that."

"And that's why she's also taking Serbo-Croatian," says Margaret. "Peter, I'm sure Harvard also knows there are plenty of upscale Slavs. Destiny darling, let's take a few minutes sometime this week to update your résumé and your Web site."

The following morning at Starbucks, Margaret meets Cynthia Ravachevsky, a friend of forty with a son of five and a daughter of four, both of whom already may be lost. Over latte, Cynthia pours out her heart with her cream.

"Maggie, how did you get *through* it?" she says. "Brian has interviews at Park Avenue Christian, Trevor Day, *and* Bank Street this week, and I don't know whether to give him Prozac or Ritalin. Which one is for morning interviews?"

"For the Upper East Side, I'd go with Paxil. Cyn, I thought you had All Souls Unitarian too."

"Please, I'm *sick* about that. I was *late*: A message on their machine said all 150 applications are already out. You'd think Unitarians would be warmer than that."

"They've always been strange," says Margaret. "They don't think Jesus was anything special. How's Brian's studying been going?"

"We've been cramming animals, numbers, colors, species, and where his navel is. What else do they want him to show?"

"Well, offhand, his ability to benefit from new experiences, his feeling for the environment, his mental balance, his talent for leadership, and not peeing in his pants. A child can be a little Aristotle, but a few drops will still ruin him."

"Maggie, do you think I should paint his thumb so he won't suck it while giving mature answers?"

"No admissions office likes a painted thumb; it makes them wonder about self-reliance. You know what Ellie's daughter said at the Emanu-El interview?"

"An Elizabethan sonnet?"

"That of course, but also 'fuck you.'"

"That sinks her."

"Oh no: She said it to her mother, not the interviewer, so it showed independence, and vocabulary, too."

"What would've sunk her would be a crayon-holding disability. Audrey's daughter has one and she's suicidal."

"Audrey or the daughter?"

"Both."

"Maggie, I don't know what I'll *do* if Brian doesn't make it!"

"You'll find the strength to go on, the way the Turks did after the earthquake. Where else have you applied?"

"Everett, Temple Emanu-El, Trinity, Madison Avenue Presbyterian, Fieldston, Chapin, and Rudolf Steiner."

"Forget Steiner; it's harder than All Souls—just to get an *interview*. Well, wherever he goes, you'll need a second mortgage. You know, Trevor Day is twenty thousand."

"They're *all* twenty thousand. That's why we can't be judgmental about the families that are selling drugs. I envy the Colombians. *They* don't have to apply for financial aid."

"You know, *I* made a terrible mistake with Destiny, because I was distracted by my abortion after that thing with the Culligan man. Destiny is . . . well, she's *six* and still at a *public* school."

"I know; I haven't told anyone. People get *pregnant* in public schools. Even worse, they lead to the wrong colleges."

"That's why we're trying for the transfer to Dalton—her best shot for Harvard. She'd get pregnant there by someone I'd want to have in my home."

"Maybe she and Allison will be schoolmates. Allison has a Dalton interview too. Same advice on what to prepare for?"

"Well, at four she has to show social sophistication, like not spitting at anyone or rolling on the floor or throwing blocks or laughing about penises."

"I've had Brian showing her his penis for years; she's stopped laughing. I'm really worried about the part where they watch her play; I'm not sure she knows how. Are there tutors for that?"

"Well, cramming for play is a tricky—"

"Maggie, have I done *enough*?"

"Does she have a Little Language Doll?"

"She already knows some Spanish and French."

"No, the one that speaks Mandarin Chinese. What they speak at Beijing Day."

"I'll get one. She *does* have the Growing Smart laptop."

"Kids in *Haiti* have *that*. How are your letters of recommendation?"

"I have one from Tom Cruise."

"Make sure you let them know how Cruise knows the child. Phyllis made a bad mistake with that letter from George W. Bush. How's your parent's essay?"

"It worries me. You know that question, *What are her special interests, talents, and abilities?* Well, some of what I wrote is actually *true* and it just may not sound strong enough."

"Don't worry, the parent's essay is just one thing. The entrance exam is much more important. The old ERB."

"Elaine has a tutor for the ERB from Ivywise Kids. To help William with the questions and the puzzles. The essay, of course, is all hers. Was yours easy to do?"

"No, but that's because I wrote it in iambic."

"Why didn't I think of that! Listen, there's one question on the ERB: *How would your child spend a free hour?*"

"And you said . . . "

"He *has* no free hours."

"*Perfect;* it's a trick question: they want to catch you with a hole in the schedule."

"Still . . . sometimes I wake up in the middle of the night and see them both at the Kelman School of Refrigeration. And I get so discouraged by all the foolish things being written. At Elizabeth Arden I saw an article by a doctor named Cotton that said, *The emotional development of children depends on imaginative play.* What the hell does he mean by *that?* I've had *both* the kids in imaginative plays—Allison was Lady Macbeth in *Tragedies for Tots*—and I think Shakespeare is *goddamn* developing, don't you?"

"Don't let Cotton pull the wool over your eyes," says Margaret.

"Oh, I *needed* that!" says Cynthia with a smile. "I'm just so *tense*. But if anyone has a breakdown, I hope it's me and not the kids."

"We *all* do. And if the kids break down, it certainly doesn't have to go on their résumés."

"You know, Brian's résumé may be a bit light in intellectual competition. I wish he had something else besides chess."

"Brian shows remarkable maturity for five. If he weren't so short, I might forget he's a child. Just don't let either of them take blankets into the interviews. Sally's boy . . . he knew all his fractions and how to draw the alimentary canal, but he ran over to Sally's bag, pulled out his blinky, and smothered Harvard, Yale, and Duke with it. And *don't* let Brian mention Barney. He's too old to be watching a prehistoric nitwit."

"Sarah Golden is using a tutor *and* a psychologist for Jeffrey's interviews. The shrink is $300 an hour."

"But isn't that what any mother in the *world* would do? Well, maybe not the Filipinos."

"Will you be using any artificial intelligence?"

"Not for preschool; just breast implants for her graduation. I'm keeping her *mind* real."

That evening at dinner, after asking Destiny for a review of the Dreyfus case, Margaret says, "Sweetie, will you be sleeping tonight or Instant Messaging?"

"I'll just be going online for some trading," says Destiny. "I want to help you two with the Dalton tuition."

Peter's eyes start to tear as he says, "We must have done *something* right: This child is a saint!"

"Never call her a *child*," says Margaret, "*or* a saint. Do you want her turned down because the school has enough immature Catholics?"

"I thought we were Jewish," says Destiny.

"We *could* be, sweetie. Let's play it by ear at the interview."

"Jesus was Jewish."

"Mention that only at Ethical Culture. All right, as long as we're on it, *name* all the disciples, all the apostles, and all the popes who had children."

There was only one question that Destiny, Brian, Jeffrey, Allison, and Melanie never would be asked: What year did common sense die?

If they were asked that question, no one would care about the answer, because Americans have become uneasy with common sense. People wonder about the fathers of female tennis players, but those men have lost their marbles in the American mainstream, which is chock-full of marbles now.

In one television commercial, a father is firing tennis balls from a machine at a daughter who looks about two. After he has assaulted her with guided missiles for a few seconds, a voice says, "How are you going to finance *your* retirement?" One hopes that the girl learns to play well enough to pay for both her daddy's retirement *and* the reconstruction of her psyche.

This commercial would have been merely comic in the days before the rise of push-parenting, the days before parents were telling first-grade teachers to give their children more homework.

One mother told me that she was sending her third-grade son to summer school to improve his math.

"He failed it?" I asked her.

"No," she said, "he got a B-plus, and that's certainly not good enough."

And you could use a summer school for parenting, I thought. Right now, you're qualified only for cocker spaniels.

"These parents are the scariest I've ever seen," one first-grade teacher told me. "They don't want children, they want little adults."

These parents want peers. They are little adults themselves.

6

The Way We Were

Shakespeare almost said, "Play's the thing," but a prominent psychiatrist named Alvin Rosenfeld did say, "Play doesn't just make kids happy and healthy, it also makes them smarter, because it refreshes and stimulates the mind. Einstein was a dreamer." Einstein's mother let the kid go glasssy at meals and she let him bounce around the bricks of Ulm with no trips to classes in dueling, beer making, or how to invade France.

There was once a time in America when a kid's only schedule was sunrise and sunset, when every day for a kid was a day at the improv. There was once a time when your mother knew only that you were playing outside and your father wasn't sure what zip code you were in; but both of them knew that they would eventually see you again, probably in the next day or two for a meal.

A kid today, who has a curriculum instead of a childhood, who has never known the heady feeling of actually
making his own plans, *still* often says, "I'm bored."

I cannot remember these two words ever spoken by me
or my friends in the merry unscheduled days of my own
American boyhood, when the domino effect was no more a
metaphor for good schools than was Chinese checkers.
From time to time, when I see children who every day are
being transported through a loop of enrichment, I think
longingly of a time when I could sit for a couple of hours on
a brownstone's steps and talk of shortstops, quarterbacks,
and nipples, a time when the only recreational structure for
a kid was a traffic light in center field.

"Hindu! Hindu!" was the cry that I heard at nine o'clock on
a spring Saturday morning as I ran out into the West Side
street, but I didn't look for a man with a snake. I looked at
eight boys who were playing stickball and I understood the
cry: One of the bases was driving away.

"It woulda been *fair!*" cried a red-headed boy with glasses as he ran to the place the car had left and lunged at it
with the broomstick that was his bat. "The fender was right
here! Goddamnit, *fair ball!*"

"You're outa your mind, Morey," said a tall, muscular boy
who was standing on the manhole called second base.

"Freddie's right," said a beefy blond boy to Morey. "His
two eyes are better'n your four."

"What can *you* see, Howie," said Morey, "with your head
so far up your ass?"

"Okay, okay," said Freddie, "it's a Hindu and we take it over. Back o' the Chevy is the new first."

"The fender or the bumper?" said Howie.

"The *fender*, you horse's ass. How you gonna touch the *bumper?* You gonna hook slide into *first?* Even if it *wasn't* cement."

Bouncing the spaldeen a couple of times, Freddie now prepared to pitch to Morey, who stood at home manhole with his bat cocked above his mastoid scar and his feet close together like Stan Musial's.

"Come on, Morey!" cried a boy with a sleepy look, who sat on a Hudson just behind home. "Send it three sewers, babe!"

"No hitter, Freddie! No hitter!" cried the beefy boy from the power alley near the Chinese laundry.

About thirty feet above him, a huge woman with hair like steel wool leaned from a brownstone window and cried in a voice of Eastern Europe, "Shut up, you booms! Shut up, you stinkpots! Shut up dat noise or I call cops!"

Across the street, another woman leaned from a high brick bleacher seat and sent a warmer suggestion to one of the players:

"Beanie, don't get *killed!* You watch those cars—you *hear?*"

The boy on the Hudson looked up to her and wearily said, "F' Crissake, Ma, you see me gettin' killed?"

"Isn't that beautiful?" said a boy with horn-rimmed glasses leaning on the Hudson's fender. "She wants you back."

On this Manhattan street where my family had just moved, I watched these boys playing stickball on that April morning of 1945 and I dreamed of hitting a drive to the far side of Amsterdam Avenue; but first I would have to get into the game and I feared that the boys wouldn't like me or even believe I was almost twelve. At four feet ten and ninety-six pounds, and with a voice that belonged in *Little Women*, I could have passed for eight.

While Morey awaited the pitch, I wondered how to introduce myself; and each reply I imagined made me feel even smaller.

Hi, I'm Ralphie Schoenstein. Could you guys use another?

You think four-against-four is uneven? Or maybe you're counting Beanie's two heads.

Hi, I'm Ralphie Schoenstein. You guys live around here?

No, we live in Kansas City. We just come here for the game.

Every line that came to me triggered an answer that made me wish I was still living on Ninety-seventh Street, where I was an established member of one of New York's thousands of very little leagues, whose only organizing principle was the theft of someone's mother's broom or the handle of her carpet sweeper. While we staged asphalt versions of baseball, apartments gathered dust.

"Man, did that *drop*," said Beanie, admiring Freddie's strikeout pitch.

"*Anybody* can make a spaldeen drop," said Morey, walking away from the plate in disgust. "That's what it *does*."

"You'd need two more eyes to hit a melon," said Freddie as his team came in to bat.

"Up yours with gauze," said Morey, who had guts to say such a line to the strongest boy on the street, even though rising gauze would not have bothered someone like Freddie.

He was the first up for his team, and he stood at bat like DiMaggio: his feet far apart, his head still, and his bat held high. His fly was open, too, but all the rest of him had DiMaggio's cool command. The boy with horn-rimmed glasses pumped and pitched, and then came the sweetest sound I knew: the pop of a broomstick redirecting the hollow pink rubber ball that was called a spaldeen.

Freddie's hit was a cannon shot at the apartment house that contained the left-field seats. It just missed dramatically opening a window and instead ricocheted from high bricks toward Morey, who was staggering around looking skyward, trying to play the carom the way Mel Ott played it at the Polo Grounds; but Ott never had to avoid baby carriages coming from the bullpen.

In the only maternal supervision that came to any of us, Morey's mother cried from her bleacher seat, "Maurice, watch the *cars!*" However, improvising as every boy did in those days, Morey nimbly sidestepped a parked Plymouth and backed into a passing baby carriage. It wasn't teaching a baby how to read, but it *was* getting him into the national pastime.

Meanwhile, Freddie was triumphantly rounding the bases, from fender to manhole to fender to manhole, while the ball flew east across Amsterdam Avenue. It was a home run that left me in awe, for it had gone almost three sewers on the fly, plus an intersection on the roll, and Morey was chasing it with added incentive because a mother was chasing him. When his own mother saw him crossing Amsterdam against the light, she almost took the fast way down to the street, but I knew he would go safely through. A city boy was like a pigeon: he always sensed a car coming at him from any direction and sidestepped it like a toreador.

By the time that Freddie reached home plate, he had become my fourth hero, just behind DiMaggio, Joe Louis, and The Shadow, and I felt a fierce desire to be friends with this boy who had just hit a spaldeen as far as DiMaggio or Ott or The Shadow could have hit it. Of course, The Shadow would have been hard to pitch to and probably would have drawn a walk.

I was savoring this moment and Morey was bringing back the spaldeen from another part of town when a sharp splat suddenly startled me and I turned to see the boys dancing back from the spot where the woman with the steel-wool hair had just dumped a pail of steaming water from her window.

"You *booms!*" she cried. "People trying to *sleep!* I call the *cops!*"

As the boys retreated toward me, Freddie looked up at her and cried, "Why dontcha sleep at night like everyone else, ya big fat bitch?"

His tongue was as awesome as his bat.

After disappearing for a few seconds, the woman returned with more refreshment, but the targets were now out of range, gathered beside the DeSoto where I also was standing.

"I guess the game's been called on account of rain," I heard myself say, hoping that Freddie might be amused and recognize my existence; but in spite of my eloquence, I remained invisible.

"Let's throw some water *back*," said Beanie.

"You gonna throw it three floors *up?*" said Freddie.

"Water grenades. Water bombs that we toss up."

"Beanie, you got an IQ?"

"Hey, I bet she's a Nazi," said a boy I soon learned was Sidney.

"No, she sounds Hungarian to me," I found the nerve to say, and all the faces turned toward this uninvited mouth. "I mean, my grandmother's Hungarian and . . . and—well, of course, it could be a different *part* of Hungary—or maybe Spain."

I wished I had been The Shadow now, but I had finally engaged them and I couldn't stop.

"By the way, I'm Ralphie Schoenstein."

Five of them said "Hi." By a majority vote, I was recognized.

"Hey, if I get another guy, can I play?"

"Where do you see another guy?" said Freddie.

"What about him?" I said, pointing to a silver-haired man in a purple shirt.

"Herman only plays if the other team has a bookie, too."

"All of us been living here for about fifty years," said Morey. "You shoulda come then."

"It would *still* be an odd number," said a boy who was Buddy.

"Ah, let him play," said Howie. "Freddie equals two guys."

The suspense of their decision stilled my tongue, but not Freddie's. Suddenly he launched a big glistening bubble into the air, a trick I couldn't believe; I had always thought I was the only boy in America who could do it.

"He's the only one in the universe who can do that without eating soap," said Buddy.

"No, listen: I can do it, *too!*" I said, and then tried a launching of my own, but nerves had dried my saliva and I merely seemed to be facing a dentist. I had always bubbled brilliantly at home, a talent my father had called gifted spitting and one that had moved my grandmother to say, "His mouth is like a washing machine." Now, however, while I kept sweeping my tongue in dry desperation, Freddie was producing bubble after bubble to the cheers of his fans. Could any Play Station have transported them to such icky ecstasy?

"Forget it, Ralphie," said Morey. "Somethin' like that comes from God."

This is your chance! I told myself, almost exploding from the pressure. You can *spit* your way into this gang! Listen, God, if you're really involved in spit, let me let one fly!"

And then I knew that even idiotic prayers are sometimes answered: I finally managed to produce what I knew would be seen as a moist miracle. It was hardly a bubble to write to Lever Brothers about, but it filled me with wild elation while the boys watched it float down and then glisten wondrously on the sidewalk for at least two seconds.

"Jesus," said Buddy reverently, "he can do it, too."

"Of course, your stuff is small and it needs height," Freddie told me. "You do anything else, Ralphie? I mean, like piss over the top of a car? Beanie can do that."

"Just Studebakers," said Sidney.

"*Anything* but a truck!" cried Beanie proudly, his right hand dropping to his zipper like a West Side gunfighter.

"No pissin' *now*, goddamnit, we're *playin'!*" said Freddie, who then turned to me and said, "Okay, you can play with them."

"You play deep center," said Morey.

"How deep?" I asked him.

"Across the street," he said with a laugh.

"Cut the shit, Morey," said Freddie. "He stays on this side of Amsterdam."

"Gee, thanks," I said, grateful for being allowed to play a position that was in the neighborhood.

Moments later I nervously took my place at the manhole just before Amsterdam and looked up to study the houses on both sides of the street to see if I could predict the caroms that might be coming to me. However, all I could predict was that I had a good chance of falling into one of the cellars that lay at the bottom of steep stone steps on both sides of the left and right field sidewalks. I wondered if anyone would have noticed if I suddenly disappeared.

As Howie came to bat, I spread my legs, bent my knees a bit, and peered hard toward the distant home plate, the way that real outfielders did. I might not have been able to detect a spaldeen flying out to me, but at least I would see any car that crossed the field from the Broadway end because the field was a one-way street. In fact, my mother need not have worried about my playing deep center field because four other boys would have had to be run down before my turn arrived. What my mother and I didn't know was that police cars could come in either direction; and so, the one that suddenly stopped beside me caught our boys in a sneak attack that was hardly the American way being fought for by boys on other fields.

"Okay, let's have the stick," said one of the cops.

Freddie had already thrown the stick into the bushes of the third-base building, and the others had struck casual poses of curbside conversationalists.

"What's the charge, Officer?" I said.

"A racket that's keeping people from sleeping," he replied while the players slowly came to his car, with Freddie working on a cocky little smirk.

"But the only people who should be sleeping now are in China," I said, and some of the boys laughed.

"What're you, a comical midget?" said the cop. "I'm takin' *your* name first."

"He's new around here," said his partner, "but the rest of 'em know damn well that ball playing is for the park."

"Okay, midget," said the first cop, "let's have your name."

"Joseph Dzhugashvili," I said, trying not to laugh.

"Joseph *what?*"

"Dzhu-gash-vili. Believe me, I'd rather be Mel Ott."

"Don't be smart, Joseph; just give it to me slow," he said, and slowly I gave him Stalin's old name.

Following my lead, the eight other boys then gave names that they felt were more fitting for the occasion than their own. When he had finished his list of fictional characters, the first cop said, "One last chance, that's what I'm givin' ya. I'm gonna letcha keep the stick this time, but the next complaint we get about this goddamn game, we're takin' more than just your names."

As the cops drove off, Freddie turned to me with a smile and said, "Ralphie, that was *great*."

"Thanks," I said, feeling as good as if I had hit for three sewers.

"Yeah, givin' that phony Italian name, that was terrific," said Beanie.

"It's not Italian; it's Stalin's real name."

"No kiddin'," said Morey. "I shoulda given 'em Hirohito instead of Mike McGee."

"Well, at least you guys gave 'em phony names, too," I said.

"Phony for us, but real for our elevator men," said Freddie. "Did you *hear* that stupid cop? He's gonna let us keep the stick! Fuckin' right he is, 'cause he don't feel like searchin' the whole *West Side* for it!"

And then the nine of us laughingly spread out on the field to continue the happiest crime I knew.

In the bottom of the eighth inning, while I was playing my profoundly deep center field, Freddie connected again, but with too much uppercut, and hit a fly so high that I lost sight of it for a couple of seconds; and then, trying to get under the ball as it drifted toward a building, I staggered backward across the sidewalk and through the open door of a Chinese laundry, to become the first man in stickball history ever to chase a fly indoors. When the laundryman asked me for my ticket, I was reminded again that my sporting destiny might not be a glorious one. I knew that even when he was twelve, DiMaggio always went for the ball and never his boxer shorts.

7

Good Old Golden Drool Days

It has always seemed to me that a child should learn to read at the age of one only if he is taking a driving test. Of course, I am not an authority on reading, only on malted milks, stickball, and the metaphysical depths of the Three Stooges. However, I sleep with a woman who teaches reading at an elementary school. When I told her that I was about to visit a place that taught parents how to teach reading to children of one, she said, "Why not teach them something more useful, like catching crocodiles? You know, in Denmark they don't start formal reading instruction until seven."

"Then we can kick Danish butt in literacy," I said.

"No, we can't. The age when you learn to read has absolutely no bearing on how well you'll do it. But teaching reading at one must have been popular with the Puritans because it's a nice way to make mothers feel guilty when they find their kids can't do it. They blame themselves and they also see the kids as not capable and lower their expectations for them."

"Wow, a double-header: ruins *both* generations."

"But not the psychiatrists the kids have to see later."

A few days later I went to a school near Philadelphia that felt Fun for Ones was too playfully useless for creating a Superkid, a place that claimed to produce readers who were not yet able to hold up a book, a place with a name that made the name Harvard College sound frivolous: The Institutes for the Achievement of Human Potential.

The director of the Institutes, a physiotherapist named Glenn Doman who founded it in 1955, had said, "Any child at birth has the potential of Einstein. By six, it's too late."

Did he mean *Albert* Einstein? It was time for me to find out at this mother lode for overloading mothers. Dr. John Cotton had talked about the high-powered marketing of baby betterment. The Institutes for the Achievement of Human Potential ("Gimme an I, baby! . . . Gimme an A!") was the Home Depot of early development. I had heard psychologists say that early pressure to achieve could be disastrous, that small children pushed beyond their capacities were often pushed right into therapy; and a mother I knew had told me, "I pushed my toddler with those silly flash cards, but he didn't get brighter, just very unhappy and insecure."

But perhaps she hadn't pushed the tot properly and had aimed too low by merely trying to turn out a champion speller; or perhaps she had flashed the subjunctive to a baby who was craving the conditional. She had needed the Institutes, which possessed a wisdom beyond just the wisdom to collect $1,575 for a one-week course. The Institutes, whose director had said that every child has the potential to surpass both Einstein *and* Da Vinci, could have told this misguided woman how to launch her infant into his own Renaissance for just $220 a day.

For slightly more than half that daily rate, the Institutes sent me the basic Da Vinci designing kit: a book called *How to Teach Your Baby to Read,* a videotape called *How to Teach Your Baby to Read,* two audiotapes called *How to Teach Your Baby to Read,* a set of flash cards, sets of flash strips for single words, couplets, phrases, and sentences, a pamphlet called *Multiply Your Baby's Intelligence with Glenn Doman Books and Kits,* a registration form for several one-week courses, and an order form to buy all of this again.

Aware that I might have lacked the IQ to use this kit myself, I called the Institutes to arrange a tour and reached a Dr. Neil Harvey, who said, "Is there a specific reason why you want to visit us?"

"Oh yes!" I replied. "I have a granddaughter who's six months old and she still can't read."

"Yes," he said with feeling, "I'm afraid there are many children like that. But it doesn't mean she's not a potential genius."

"Oh, my family has had *potential* geniuses for hundreds of years. We all haven't realized it—I guess a couple of my cousins would have to be called idiots—but my *granddaughter*—"

"She's certainly *gifted*."

"On her worst day. Most of the time, she's flat-out *superior*—you absolutely couldn't tell she's related to Hungarians—and I'm sick at the thought of her falling behind and losing her chance for Yale."

"There's still time," he said. "But before you take the Better Baby tour, you have to read either *How to Multiply Your Baby's Intelligence* or *How to Teach Your Baby to Read*."

"I probably should've read them when I was two," I said, "but I'll do it right away. If it means anything, I *did* go to Hunter College Model School for exceptional children when I was six."

"That was late to be exceptional."

"Yes, we did waste a lot of time playing kickball."

"Glenn Doman feels that a child would rather learn to read than do anything else in the world."

"I wish my mother had known that when I spent all those years playing stickball; I'd be in Mensa today. But I want my granddaughter to be a genius as quickly as possible, so I'd like to visit the Institutes—although you know, of course, there are people opposed to what you do."

"They were opposed to Galileo."

"Not the same people, but good point. What I mean is, for example, there's a preschool director in New York who says that if you teach children to read even at four, they're missing something, because children have only a certain amount of emotional energy."

"Someone like that directs a school?"

"I'm afraid that Professor David Elkind agrees with her. He says the pressure for early reading reflects the *parents'* need, not the child's."

"The child's need *is* the parents'."

"But—you mean if a child wants to eat clay, then his parents . . ."

"This Professor Ellman is from where?"

"Elkind. He's chairman of the Child Study Department at Tufts."

"Well, he'd better study some new children. And you'd better visit us and forget about Tufts."

The following Monday morning, after a weekend of trying to read *How to Teach Your Baby to Read*, I drove to a suburb of Philadelphia called Wyndmoor, entered a huge iron gate that said THE INSTITUTES FOR THE ACHIEVEMENT OF HUMAN POTENTIAL, and parked at a collection of small stone buildings that looked like a division three college. Above the outside stone wall flew the flags of several nations. I knew some of them, but the babies here probably knew them all.

Spotting a sign that pointed to the Better Baby Store, I walked over and found guides for parents who had not just the traditional great expectations but stratospheric ones: *Kids Who Start Ahead Stay Ahead*, a book for parents who felt that life was a race demanding early acceleration and not the sputtering start of someone like Winston Churchill; *How to Teach Your Baby to be Physically*

Superior, for parents unsure if just being a genius was enough; *How to Give Your Baby Encyclopedic Knowledge,* for parents who wanted college for the cradle; and *How to Teach Your Baby Math,* for parents who mistook their babies for computers.

Near the books were stacks of T-shirts, some for adults that said I'M A PROFESSIONAL MOTHER and I'M A PROFESSIONAL FATHER, and some tiny ones that said I CAN READ and I'M GONNA WIN.

For a long time I looked at I'M GONNA WIN, because those words said it all: a slogan to be flaunted by the children of the new winner-take-all America, the children whose parents saw childhood as a time to blast out of the blocks in a sixteen-year dash to an ivy-covered finish line. These parents would have laughed at the words of William Damon of Stanford University, who said of childhood, "These are supposed to be the years that kids wander around, without the pressures of the real world."

"Well, I'm certainly not sending Stanley to a preschool for Stanford!" the professional mother would have said. "Just wander around? The Israelites did that and it took them forty years to get anywhere."

In that morning's newspaper I had seen a story about the state of the I'm-Gonna-Win America that made me contemplate Romanian citizenship. In Jacksonville, Florida, a former youth program coach had been sent to jail for breaking both arms of a ten-year-old football player who had muffed a catch.

It's not just whether you win or lose, it's how quickly you heal.

After browsing in the bookstore, I left its collection of racing forms and walked to the main building to meet Tina Travers, director of the Early Development Program, for a tour. A woman of about sixty, she was a rampantly cheerful dispenser of the Gospel According to Glenn Doman.

"This place is a miracle!" she said as she began leading me down a long path. "We start the reading programs at three months, and by six months they're reading, even though they can't tell you about it."

"That happens a lot in college," I said, "so this is good preparation."

"Oh, you have a nice sense of humor. Glenn Doman believes in humor."

That was already clear from her statement of his goals.

"He founded this place in 1955?" I said.

"Yes, at first to help brain-injured children."

Such help seemed worthwhile to me, although Judy said that even *its* value was questionable. However, after initially working with brain-injured children, Doman turned to tampering with brains that *he* could injure. Dr. Margaret G. Ruddy, professor of psychology and director of Infant/Child Studies at the College of New Jersey, had agreed with the Carnegie report by telling me, "Early stimulation does matter, but Doman is giving infants the wrong kind, so he's actually depriving them of the stimulation that *counts*. The critical period for reading is *not* infancy. The best kind of infant brain stimulation is just crawling around and exploring, picking up things and being smiled at and hugged and tossed in the air."

Had Glenn Doman ever been tossed in the air? Experts were making me see that perhaps he should have been shot from a cannon.

"The Doman people feel that a stimulated brain is a smarter one," I had told Professor Ruddy before going to the Institutes.

"Not *their* stimulation," she'd replied. "Not *reading*. Reading is one of those things that's learned better later on."

Wondering if there was *any* medical confirmation for the mass production of *kleine* Einsteins and demi–da Vincis, I now said to Tina Travers, "Do you have pediatricians here who support pulling infants out of infancy this way?"

"No pediatricians," she said. "But Dr. Harvey is an Ed.D."

Thinking of the Mayo Clinic being run by an English major, I said, "I've heard that teaching babies to read too early could damage the neurons in their brains or even make them lose neurons by not having enough of the right stimulation."

"Oh no, our program *develops* neurological pathways in the baby's brain."

It was a development that she herself still might have been able to use, for she then began telling me of the physical value that creeping has for a three-month-old.

"Yes," I said, "some of them do need practice. I remember that my wife and I put our first daughter on the floor at that age and we were so upset that she just didn't go anywhere. But she still turned out well. She even has a good sense of direction."

"You were lucky, but all of us could have done so much *more,*" she said as we entered a large auditorium that reminded me of a college lecture hall. "It all happens in here. This is where the mothers take the one-week course in how to multiply their baby's intelligence."

"Not just increase but *multiply?*" I said. "A 140 IQ would become a *280?* If you're multiplying by 2, that is."

"Well, we *do* cover a tremendous amount of material in just seven days with lectures, demonstrations, and practical applications. We integrate the physical *and* the intellectual, and they just gobble it up."

"The babies or the mothers?" I said.

"The mothers."

"They bring their own babies or you hand some out?"

"We have some for demonstration. But it doesn't really matter what child you use because every child is a genius."

Every child is a genius. I thought about the hundreds of well-disguised geniuses I had known, people I unfairly had called jerks. It hadn't been *their* fault for wasting their first six months just being inarticulate blobs instead of Einsteins in bloom. I thought about my boyhood friend Beanie, who had stolen things from stores during Two-for-One sales, saying, "I take the free one." I thought about the owners of baseball teams. I thought about the governor of Minnesota.

"This is the week's schedule," she said, showing me a list of the classes for each day. They covered how to teach your baby to read, how to teach your baby math, how to give your baby encyclopedic knowledge, how to teach your baby music, and how to teach your baby a foreign language. In the early acceleration capital of the world, this was the American Dream: a child of six months doing geometry while singing *Aïda* in Bulgarian.

While Tina rhapsodized about infants being crawling encyclopedias, I pondered this national contest to see which child could be freed from childhood the fastest. Such postpartum liberation from life's most blessed state ignored the words of the Roman Juvenal: *The greatest reverence is due a child! It is a wicked act to despise your child's tender years.* Of course, how could Americans be asked to heed the advice of a man who probably had learned to read when he was X?

Because my response to catapulting a baby out of that particular state was the sentimental one of a man with merely a Columbia College B.A., I wanted the wisdom of authorities; and so, after coming home from the Institutes, I played the tape of *How to Teach Your Baby to Read* to Judy and Professor Ruddy.

"I'd rather be seeing *Singin' in the Rain*," said Judy as the tape began.

"They're teaching people to speak in this one, too," I replied.

The tape began with Glenn Doman scolding Americans because "we spend our children's first six years de-geniusing them when every child has a greater potential than Leonardo."

"He must mean DiCaprio," said Judy while Professor Ruddy merely laughed.

"Reading should start to be taught the moment a baby comes home from the hospital," said Doman, "because he'll soon learn to read from TV."

Professor Ruddy now looked like someone who was watching *Duck Soup*.

"This man is beyond belief," she said. "There's no validity to *any* of this."

"Why should you learn to read as a baby?" Glenn Doman was saying. "Because it makes you schoolproof."

This man saw school as academic asbestos, but I kept the tape running: I had to know if there was *any* sense to America's new lust for developing diapered intellectuals. As Doman went on, I saw that he was equating reading with intelligence, thus saying something about his own.

"There's no evidence that early readers are any smarter," said Professor Ruddy.

New York Times education writer Richard Rothstein had confirmed her point by saying, "Many *five*-year-olds are not ready for academics." Italics mine, but you may have them.

To show that Glenn Doman had passed his flickering torch to his daughter Janet, she now appeared on the tape to say, "A baby will regard reading as no harder than your talking to him."

"Ridiculous! Babies are *auditory*," said Professor Ruddy, while I thought of the words of H. L. Mencken: *No one ever went broke underestimating the intelligence of the American people*. Mencken knew that America was one big carnival, and now the midway was full of women who were trying to be good mothers by playing Glenn Doman's scholastic shell game.

The tape moved on to show young mothers flashing words on cards for students between three and six months old.

"Look at your child's face as you show him the words," said Janet Doman. "See if he's having a good time. If he's bored, it's your fault."

The babies in the demonstration would have had to be slightly more interested to be called bored. Every one of them looked like a poster child for Stupor.

"There's not one example here of a baby learning anything," said Judy. "Not only not reading but not even *single words*."

"And how would you even *know* when a child this age is learning a word?" said Professor Ruddy. "This is pseudo-science, totally hokey."

"Hokey" would have been an easier word for the babies to ignore than some of those the mother was flashing, like "Bathtub." Of course, even if she was taking the course at home for only $144, it was the mother who was taking the bath.

"Remember," Janet Doman was saying, "the learning curve drops at six."

Clearly, hers did, a woman who confused intelligence with the ability to read, a woman who now said, "It's important to keep in mind that you don't have to be able to *talk* to read."

I didn't need either of my two authorities to be able to think: How would you know that a voiceless baby was reading? He would have to send you an e-mail.

"A baby this age doesn't even understand *spoken* words," said Professor Ruddy. "A baby couldn't begin to read unless he understood speech, so there's no place in the baby's brain to even respond to reading."

But there was no place in Janet Doman's brain to respond to this logic.

"A child can learn to read more easily at eighteen months than later on," she now said.

"Absolutely no evidence for that," said Professor Ruddy. "And how much reading can an eighteen-month-old do if he can recognize only 'spaghetti'?"

On the tape, the mothers continued assaulting their babies with cards, some of which said SPAGHETTI, BATHTUB, and DADDY, all of which should have said I'M A MAD MOMMY. None of the babies had thrown up, but I was worried about Professor Ruddy.

"This is nauseating," she said.

"Even if you *could* teach babies to read," said Judy, "why *do* it?"

The answer would have to come from the Domans' accountant.

8

The Whole World in His Hands

I do not know what college my grandson Ned will attend. He is five years old, so any application he made now would be an early decision indeed. Ned is highly intelligent, but he is not being propelled toward any particular ivy by his parents or by Judy and me because, just like your kids, he has his own fast forward; and if an adult has any sense, he will use this speed for the joy of the moment and never for tomorrow's admission. Moreover, I am happy to say that I never use Ned for the fun of depressing other parents and grandparents, the way I did at those grim times when I went into reproductive combat.

Ned likes *Sesame Street,* but he much prefers Savannah, Sonoma, Poughkeepsie, and all the funny names in between. He is a moppet hooked on maps, which have hooked me, too, since I was his age. Driven by my own gene for enjoying geography, Ned loves to play with a jigsaw puz-

zle of the fifty states. He never tires of putting the Republic
together, which he does with the zeal of Lincoln. He also
has a little book about the states and he knows many state
facts, unaware that they are as meaningful to most
Americans today as the annual rainfall of Myanmar.

Often when I walk into Ned's house, he sounds like a
presidential candidate:

"Ralph, let's put the country together."

"Great; dump the country," I reply.

And then we spill his fifty favorite pieces on the floor
and together we form a perfect union. I go through the
motions of helping him, but he can do it alone. While he
does, I remember my own boyhood delight in assembling a
puzzle of forty-eight balsa-wood states. I was in love with
such sounds as San Luis Obispo, Tallahassee, Sheboygan,
Texarkana, Walla Walla, Azusa, Kokomo, and Kalamazoo.
And how wonderful it was that the capital of South Dakota
had the same name as my uncle Pierre. Might I also have
had a relative named Portland, like Fred Allen's wife? For a
Jewish boy, there could be no St. Paul, of course; but
Helena was possible. I hadn't yet learned that King Lear
hung out with a guy named Albany.

The romance that I found in the map of the United
States so enchanted me that, while other boys were putting
on Little League uniforms, I was savoring how Florida and
Oklahoma managed to fit their panhandles so neatly into
slots just below Alabama and just above Texas. Today, more
than fifty years later, I still get a kick out of the way that
Missouri manages to touch eight other states; and I enjoy

asking Ned questions that will not be part of his entrance exam for a trendy kindergarten.

"Hey, Ned," I say, handing him Montana, "what's the country right above this one?"

"Canada, of course," he replies.

"And what's the capital?"

"Canada isn't a state. It doesn't have a capital."

"No, I mean the capital of this little rectangle."

"Hel-leeena," he says with a patronizing smile. "Everyone knows *that*."

I do not tell him there are people in Montana who do not know that, and people in Kansas who think the capital of Montana is Butte, and people in Maine who think it is Little Big Horn. Ned will learn too soon that he is spinning his globe to a different drummer, that learning geography is now as important to most Americans as learning the prime ministers of Peru.

A few years ago a *National Geographic* survey revealed that 25 percent of the high school students in Texas couldn't name the country that bordered them on the south. Many of the others, however, knew it was Bolivia.

"Want to hear something funny, Ned?" I say as he snaps in California. "Sacramento is a tomato juice."

"That's silly," he says. "Sacramento is the capital of California."

"Well, at least Tropicana isn't the capital of Hawaii."

"Where's Tropicana, Ralph?"

His questions are harder than mine; and while I try to come up with an answer for this one, I watch his sure little hands moving pieces that trigger memories.

New Mexico ... when I almost came to blows with another fourth-grader because he kept insisting that the capital of New Mexico was Albuquerque and I kept telling him it was Santa Fe. Can you imagine two fourth-graders today fighting about Olympia?—only about whether synchronized swimming should be allowed.

Tennessee ... when I tried to test the accuracy of the lyrics of "Chattanooga Choo-Choo" (*You leave the Pennsylvania Station 'bout a quarter to four / Read a magazine and then you're in Baltimore*) by finding a magazine that could last a reader all the way from New York to Baltimore. I finally decided it would have to be the *Congressional Record*.

Nevada ... when I had the thrill of discovering that Reno was *west* of Los Angeles. How marvelous: part of the West Coast was actually *east* of something! I couldn't wait to drop this dramatic news into a conversation, but the longitude of Reno rarely came up in my neighborhood. At last, at a high school dance, I blurted it out to a young lady, who wasted no time leaving me for a boy with a New York state of mind.

Nebraska ... when I stumbled on another astounding fact with a similar power to anesthetize: Nebraska is the only state in the union with a unicameral legislature. Again, I tried to woo with cartographic charm, telling another young lady, "Rhoda, do you know that Nebraska has only one house?"

"You're not making any sense," she said, speaking for dozens of others. "If there's only one house in Nebraska, where does everyone in Nebraska *live?* In *sleeping bags?*"

And Oklahoma ... when I said to my sixth-grade teacher, "How can the corn in Oklahoma be as high as an elephant's eye when there are no elephants in Oklahoma?"

"Maybe the circus came and had a performance in a cornfield," she said, an answer that disappointed me. Even in 1945, the lover of geography often walked a lonely road and only he knew its coordinates.

"And so, what is New Jersey between?" I said to Ned a few days ago, not pushing him but just gently leading him into more all-American fun.

"I told you, Ralph," he replied. "New Jersey is between New York and Pennsylvania. You should remember that because we live between there."

And now, in spite of all the intense tutoring about everything from mammals to math, the road is even lonelier for someone who enjoys knowing that New Jersey still faces Portugal and that there are seventeen places in America named Princeton and that the top of Mount Washington is the best place to fly a kite, if you don't mind taking flight yourself. How sadly out of step is my bright little Ned, growing up in a country where adults want toddlers to know everything but the land where they live, a country where knowing all about its states is merely a quirky state of mind.

9

The Way We Were

When you see a play, you have to suspend your disbelief; but when you see some of the ways in which childhood is now being nipped in the bud, mere suspension will not do: Your disbelief has to be shredded. And once it is, then you can accept that PSAT has a new meaning in America: Promiscuity Starts at Ten.

That is a bit hyperbolic, of course: many children are not greeting sex until eleven or twelve. There are always late bloomers.

In early 2001, the National Center for Health reported that one child in twelve is no longer a virgin by the age of thirteen. And by the time that the kids are middle-aged, say fifteen, one-third of the girls have had sex and almost half the boys, a nice introduction for the kids to America's double standard.

In no part of accelerated America has baby been wished a heartier good-bye than in this awesome effort to awaken his sleeping little glands. Leading the way in ending the silly old celibacy of children are the stores and catalogs that are titillating people who used to come into heat only at the beach: there are bras and panties and skintight Lycra tops and slit skirts for *five*-year-olds." A bra for a five-year-old is a fetching tourniquet, of course; but just pointing a five-year-old toward any arousal besides getting out of bed would have caused shock in Sodom and Gomorrah. I cringe at the thought of Ned laughing at Intercourse, Pennsylvania.

Robin Goodman of NYU's Child Study Center says that American children now believe that oral sex is the latest sport. Will oral sex be replacing soccer? Will millions of moms be driving their kids from one gamy game to another? Shocker moms?

Every time there is an appalling new song by some rapper, we hear talk about the end of Western civilization. However, even the most primeval rapper is a champion of Western civilization when compared to sixth-graders who think that oral hygiene is brushing before a profoundly personal encounter, who think that oral sex is an intramural sport, a merry kind of chastity, a hormonal halfway house.

I'm too old to handle it, and they are too young. I come from a time when American children had neither mental nor physical command of sex, when even early teenagers were full of immaculate misconception. The week I turned twelve, Beanie, who was the same age, gave me a sexual education that was charmingly typical of that bygone time.

"It's somethin' your mother 'n' father do," he said with pithy eloquence. "Your mother 'n' father, they're definitely the ones involved."

In the summer of that year, the year I had joined the stickball game, I went to a boys' camp in Maine called Wigwam and did something that no twelve-year-old in America has done for a very long time: I fell in love with love.

That summer, I was almost four feet eleven, but still had my soprano voice and had never been kissed by anyone but my mother, my father, and two Hungarian aunts, and I was about to tell my father to find another guy. Early that July, while I eagerly awaited the first camp dance, my hungry heart lay under a T-shirt that said STUYVESANT, the high school I would enter in the fall. Because of my incomplete size, the ST and NT adorned my armpits; I should have been heading for TAFT. However, even though I had a body from Disney, my romantic fantasies were from MGM.

At last, it came: the dance with Camp Fauna, my first crack at another sex. On the walk from my bunk to a social hall called the Lodge, a boy of thirteen told me, "Man, I could really use a girl tonight."

I didn't ask him for what; I felt he was trying to impress me. Boys were always trying to impress me with what they had done to girls, as if I were the scorekeeper. Beanie once had brought me the bra of a conquest who was the same size as his mother.

They came at twilight in canoes, a flotilla of middy blouses; and when they reached the shore, I prayed that just one of them would fall for my offbeat air. I had heard that very thin men like Sinatra had the greatest sex appeal, so perhaps my visible bones would inflame her. And what lay outside them was also potentially enchanting: razor-sharp white slacks, a billowy white shirt that gave the appearance of a torso beneath it, and a soaring pompadour that had taken ten minutes to set—time well spent, for I was now five feet. I exuded the promise of puberty.

While the Fauna girls climbed the hill from the beach, my counselor, Rah-Rah Rappaport, gave us the kind of talk that inspired teams to come back in the second half.

"Now, don't you guys be shy just because you're the smallest," he said. "Hell, there was a guy in France named Taloo Lautrec who used to drive women nuts and he was always looking *up* at 'em. As long as you're over four feet, you can score, so be gutsy little lovers in there tonight. Just remember to drop her hand as soon as it gets soggy. Nothin' kills romance like a soggy mitt. Okay guys, go *get* 'em!"

Some grim and some giggly, the girls marched into the Lodge, where they lined up along the wall. In size place and shorts, they looked like runty Rockettes. On the opposite wall, the boys made the same formation, and I gazed across at my female counterpart, the fourth girl in line.

She was hardly a centerfold, or even a subscription card. Not only was she full of freckles, but she could have passed for nine; she looked like a doll with measles; so I scanned the rest of the line for something worth sweeping off her feet. The problem, however, wasn't *her* feet but *mine:* I was a smooth dancer if the girl in my arms was my mother, perhaps the only female who could follow the monsterlike box step she had taught me.

"Welcome, Fauna squaws!" said Rah-Rah from the center of the lodge. "May this be a happy hunting ground for all. May our dancing please Manitou and bring rain to the crops."

The only crops at Wigwam were poison ivy, but this was a night for dreams.

"And now let's break ranks for a Paul Jones!" he said. "Braves in a circle outside, squaws inside. When the music stops, the one you're facing is yours for the first dance. Okay, you redmen, let's circle those gorgeous wagons!"

And then I saw her: a girl with dark bangs, big eyes, and teeth with a slight overbite: a mini Gene Tierney! And above all this allure was something that alone would have made my heart turn over: she was my height.

As the Paul Jones began, I kept trying to track this vision and hoping to end up as her partner; but when the music stopped, she was lost to Roger Scobbo. My spirits sank. At once I decided to cut in and courageously crossed the floor to Roger and this black-banged beauty. With a hand already damp, I tapped him on the shoulder and said, "May I?"

He smiled a gracious *Up yours* and left.

"Hi, I'm Ralph Schoenstein," I said, encircling her waist with a shaky arm.

"Hi," she said. "I'm Gloria Esposito."

To the strains of "You'll Never Know," she began to follow my box step with the tracking skill of my mother, and she smiled a smile that activated every part of her face: Her mouth sliced nearly to her ears, her nose wrinkled, her cheeks rose, and her teeth shone like Chiclets. This had to be love. A few weeks earlier I had brushed the left breast of an eighth-grade blonde in a hall at school, thinking *that* was the real thing; but now I knew it had been merely a passing fancy.

"If I happen to kick you," I said, "don't think it's personal."

She laughed so sweetly that I pulled her closer, though I still didn't dare go cheek-to-cheek like the older guys. However, some of her hair went into my mouth, and it was delicious.

"You're Italian, aren't you?" I said, debonairly spitting out a tasty strand while showing her that I had a serious side.

"Esposito usually is," she said.

"Well, it could be Spanish or even Basque," I said, squaring another of my endless boxes. I gave the remark the authority I often gave to a guess. I could be quite impressive when I didn't know what I was talking about.

"Bass?" she said.

"No, *Basque*. They live in the Pyrenees and no one knows where their language comes from."

"Gee, you've got a terrific mind."

"Thanks; I try to keep it that way."

I hoped she was falling in love with it; my body certainly wasn't going to enslave her with desire.

Suddenly I felt a tap on my shoulder: it was Wally Krantz, who had beaten me out for second base on the Wigwam junior varsity.

"May I?" he said with a maddening grin.

"If you want," I said.

Of *course* he wanted. That was why he'd asked, the little shit.

"I shall return," I said, perhaps a bit pompously, and then I walked to the wall in self-pity.

"Yours was a cute one," said Bobby Brant.

"I know," I said glumly. "And look who's got her now."

"But you can beat him *here*. He doesn't know half the words *you* do."

"You're right; I'm goin' back!" And then the music changed to "Bésame Mucho." "Damn, a *rumba*; it won't fit my box." But my drive to win Gloria was so strong that, heedless of the dismaying beat, I went back to her.

"I have returned," I said with all the charm of Douglas MacArthur.

She laughed as sweetly as before, while Wally left with a glare.

"Care to dance?" I said.

"I'd love to," she replied.

"We can skip the introductions."

She laughed again. She seemed to laugh at everything I said. Either she was in love or there was something wrong with her. But this was no time for insight, not when I was faking a rumba with someone I adored. Or was it a tango? All I knew for certain was that this was the girl for me; and so I grew even bolder and began turning my squares into rectangles. I could have made octagons, for I was intoxicated to realize that this flower of Fauna *wasn't* my height but a full half inch *shorter*.

"Where are you from?" I said, making sure I had her attention by giving her a kick in the shin. "Sorry."

"Teaneck, New Jersey," she said.

"That sounds lovely."

"My father's an adjuster there."

This strange transition led to our first lull. I was afraid to ask what her father adjusted, for stupidity could have broken the spell.

"Do you like camp?" I finally said.

"This is just my first year," she replied.

Her flair for non sequitur was defeating my mouth, so I returned to New Jersey.

"What grade are you in?"

"I'm going into the eighth."

"I'm going to Dartmouth."

"That's wonderful. When?"

"Right after high school." I kicked her again. "Sorry."

"You're a very strong dancer," she said.

This second kick gave me an inspired idea: why stay inside and destroy her legs when I could be out on the porch necking like the older boys? And out there I would also be safe from Wally and all other poachers.

"Wanna grab a little night air?" I said.

"I'd love to," she replied.

"Swell!"

Elatedly, I shoved her from the room with a gallant hand on her kidneys, hoping that Wally and Rah-Rah were watching me. I still could not believe my luck: to have conquered this beauty during ten bars of "Bésame Mucho." But why not? Romeo had needed only ten seconds to conquer Juliet, and he was my age—well, just two years older.

I wondered about Gloria's age. As an eighth-grader, she was probably twelve, but she could have been fifteen, because she didn't seem too bright. In fact, had her brain been in a boy, she would have been Beanie; but I knew that such a brain made a woman more desirable. What woman was a mental giant except Eleanor Roosevelt? Gloria Esposito was all I had ever dreamed of: an older, shorter, beautiful laugher who made me see the vision in *Laura*.

On the dark porch of the Lodge, I led her to a bench, where I tenderly took her hand and said, "You know, this part of Maine looks a little like Oregon, especially at night."

"Have you ever been to Oregon?" she said.

"Not really."

Not really? Was her mind *catching?*

"Hey, I betcha don't know the *capital* of Oregon," I said.

"I don't," she said. "I never really think about it."

"I betcha think it's Portland, same as Maine."

"I bet somebody wants me to *saaay* it's Portland."

I wondered if her teasing meant that she cared; I had heard that teasing came with love.

"It's Salem," I said, suddenly ashamed for having made her look dumb, although she could do that nicely by herself. In silent apology I squeezed her hand, transferring some sweat.

If you want this prize, I was thinking, you'd better give her something besides a geography exam.

Summoning all my courage, I said, "Has anyone ever told you you're a very pretty girl?"

Since one of the first cavemen had wondered if he should say something endearing while dragging his beloved home, no trite words had ever been spoken more often than these. My tongue was golden with latitudes, but leaden for love.

"Why, thank you," she said instead of the answer I deserved: Yes, 296 people have told me, but none as big a schmuck as you.

She was strangely soulful now: she hadn't laughed in almost two minutes. To sustain her mood I needed something poetic, but all that came to me was *I love you*, and that one I wanted to save. At last I softly said, "Do you know that your initials are the same as General Electric's?"

"Who's he?" she replied. "I haven't been following the war."

I wanted to tell her that, like the other GE, she lit up my world, but I was having my own power failure. For inspiration I looked out at the lake, and I suddenly thought of the nude sunbathing I had done on the raft with my bunkmates last week and of the Fauna canoes that had passed by. In dismay, I dropped her hand, which had been floating in mine.

"Is something wrong?" she said.

"Oh, it's really nothing." If we were to be lovers, there could be no secrets, but my confession was coming hard. "I was just wondering if . . . oh, better forget it."

"Okay."

"You've ever seen me without my clothes? Sunbathing on the raft, that is."

When she said she hadn't, I heard bells. I could woo this jewel with the thought that, no matter how skeletal my body might be, it would still be a surprise for her. She was looking at me uneasily now; my last question might have left her more flustered than the capital of Tennessee; so I lunged through the dark, missed her hand, and squeezed her wrist in a vise of reassurance.

"How'd you like to take a walk?" I said.

"I'd love to," she replied.

Was this her old reflexive reply, or did she mean it? If someone had asked her to open a vein, would she have said *I'd love to*, or would she have sliced only for me? Either way, her words were heady and I pressed on.

"How'd you like to see the boathouse?" I said, a couple of notes higher than usual.

"I'd love to."

Going to the boathouse was hardly a trip to the Taj Mahal, but it was the most romantic spot within fifty yards of the Lodge. As we started down the lawn that sloped to the lake, I nervously wondered what I would do at the boathouse. Show her boats? Or go sailing into uncharted waters?

Hand in hand, we walked silently there, and then she said, "I really love boating."

"That's great," I said. "Let's pull up a dinghy."

We went inside and sat down on one, but I left the boat-house door open, not wanting to scare her out of love.

"I wish I could row you home," I said.

She made her favorite response and I braced myself for another lull, feeling up the creek surrounded by paddles. My next line was coming hard, for I feared both making jokes and making love. If I asked her to be my girl, would she consider it the former or the latter? This was the moment to kiss her; but even *my* mouth, one of the most active in New England, lacked the power to move forward instead of just up and down.

And then, down from the Lodge, came the first strains of "Good Night, Sweetheart." I was saved.

"That's the last dance," I said.

"We better go," she replied.

Camp tradition said that your partner for the last dance became your beloved, but there wasn't time to get back to the Lodge. And so, with the mindless daring that made heroes and jackasses, too, I said, "Gloria, will you be my girl?" and blocked her answer with a kiss, which missed her lips and landed on a succulent piece of her chin.

"Ralph, *please*," she said.

Damn! At the moment that I yearned to hear those three stale little words, she had turned inventive! Please *what?* Take her back to the Lodge or be her love? She owed me an answer; and as we walked up the hill in silence and moderate mortification, I wondered if I would ever get one.

I saw her twice more that summer, but we couldn't recapture the magic of that night, perhaps because we weren't sure what the magic had been. And, of course, I could never again find the courage to ask her to be my girl or even give the capital of New Mexico. At the farewell dance in August, when "Good Night, Sweetheart" was played, she was with Wally Krantz, while I buried my broken heart in the beefy arms of Sylvia Krim.

It all seems so medieval now, a boy of twelve falling in love with love. Through all the years, I have remembered the glow of my little GE and wondered if she remembers me. When she does a crossword puzzle that asks for a state capital, does she ever think of the dapper skeleton who once whispered sweet cities in her adorable ear?

10

At Play in the Fields of the Bored

Is the Better Baby Institute, like Dr. Frankenstein's place, unique in developing potential, or are other such places now serving America's possessed parents?

The answer is the second—in fact, the second to the 300th power, for a few days after seeing the Institute, I discovered a chain of 300 Bright Start Learning Centers, a national franchise; and in the city where America was born, I went to one of them, one part of the great new movement to redesign children.

When I entered Philadelphia's Bright Start Learning Center at ten in the morning, I picked up a pamphlet called *Mission Statement*, which said, *We are committed to providing the highest quality child care, early education, and work/life solutions in the nation.*

Child care was fine and I understood it; I was trying to understand early education; but work and life solutions made no more sense to me than work and life solids. Because my mother had left my mind unfertilized for my first five years, I now had trouble translating the credo of what may or may not have been a nursery school.

There should have been clarification for me in the Center's *A Parent's Guide to Early Childhood Education*, which contained such insights as *When children put blocks in trucks and dump them out, they are learning to understand size, weight, and number concepts (math) (science). When children pretend to be grown-ups, they are learning to understand their experiences better (abstract thinking).*

Unfortunately, this second gospel did not interpret *all* the scholastic behavior of one-year-olds. It did not, for example, say: *When children throw mashed potatoes, they are learning to request boiled or fried (menu changing).*

And food *was* flying in the Goldfish Room, where eight students, each about twelve months old, were partially seated at two tables while two young women thought they were helping them to learn through play. Holding up a book, one of the women brightly said, "This is *The Big Hungry Bear* by Dan and Audrey Wood."

One of the students now gave a review of the book by spitting some cornflakes onto the table. Other students were responding to the reading with a variety of primate sounds, none of which I was able to interpret. The response of one girl, however, was clear: John and Audrey Wood had been able to move her to tears, although they probably didn't intend sobs.

Neither teacher tried to stop the child's crying and I understood why: *When a child is crying, she is learning self-expression (disgust).*

While the teacher continued to read with animation, I found myself wondering if the bear would ever get lunch. Studying the faces of the students, I found that all had a common feeling: cluelessness. It did not take T. Berry Brazelton to see that not one of them knew what was going on. Moreover, on a higher level, not one of them cared. The teacher could have been reading *The Big Hungry Bear* or a *History of Hungary*; the kids still would have been running an emotional gamut from impassive to distracted to deeply bored.

"Now, wasn't that a good book!" the reading teacher said, primarily to herself, while her associate wiped up cornflakes.

"Remember," the second teacher said, "we have a library date on Friday."

I sensed that most of the students might not have known what a *library* was. Or what *Friday* was. Or *we*.

And equally foreign may have been the noun in the first teacher's comment after she had sung "Down by the Station."

"Oh oh," she said, "*danger*."

Looking at this academic reducto ad absurdum, I thought the same thing.

While a couple of the students began to squirm and one of them began grinning at me, the second teacher sang,

"Good morning, Lydia, how are you?" to one girl, and then she sang personal greetings to the other seven; but these were kids who valued their privacy, for none of them said how he or she was. The first teacher, however, responded, and I was glad to hear that she was happy to be in Philadelphia today.

And now, as the first teacher sang, "Who has come to school today?" the second one gave all the children paper letters for their first initials: Josie, Grace, Melissa, Xavier, Allison, Colin, Melody, and Frank. Deciding to postpone literacy for five or six years, Josie, Grace, Allison, Frank, and Melissa tossed their letters aside, but Xavier was hungry for language and began to eat his.

When a child eats his letter, he is digesting whole language (lawsuit).

While one of the teachers quickly kept the X from marking Xavier's intestine, Grace burst into tears, and I felt a little blue myself.

"Does anyone know what today is?" the first teacher said.

A tough question for the students; I wasn't sure *I* could answer it. What *was* today? The anniversary of the Battle of Lake Erie? Of South Dakota becoming a state? Grover Cleveland's birthday?

"Today is Tuesday, March 20," she said. "And that's the first day of . . . ?"

Again the students were silent; they hadn't expected a quiz today; they had been preparing for the midterm.

"Today is the first day of . . . *spring*."

The pressure of an oral had been too much for Frank, and he got up and walked over to me.

"I didn't know it either," I told him. "I figured it was history, not current events."

For a few seconds he just smiled at me, lost like all the others in his own happily unenriched world. I wanted to give him a hug, but it would have had no educational value. Perhaps I was reading too much into his expression, but it seemed to be saying, I need more than Ritalin to get through this.

While the first teacher began singing about a fire station down the street, the students demonstrated every known variety of inattention. For some reason, they were not engaged by

> There's a fire station down the street,
> And the fire chief's name is Pete.
> When someone calls 911.
> All the firemen and women run.

Imposing *any* kind of structure on people who were twelve months old struck me as a national need for calling 911 and saying, "This is an emergency. America has invented a new kind of child abuse."

After the song, the teacher dumped out a box of blocks in animal shapes.

This is more like it, I thought. This is what they *should* be doing. I didn't realize, however, that the blocks were not for playing: They were a zoology quiz.

"Now, where's the iguana?" the first teacher said.

Like many of America's preschoolers who'd been trying to get footing on the fast track, these eight had been studying the wrong things, probably frogs or infectious diseases, because no one knew what an iguana was. There may be twelve-month-old children who say *iguana*, but *I wanna* is probably what they're going for.

A few minutes later the second teacher moved the kids from their tables to the floor, where they formed a circle.

That's more natural for them, I thought, while one boy sank into the teacher's lap.

But now, instead of just playing with the kids, she pulled another surprise quiz. Pointing to some toy kitchen supplies, she said, "Where is the utensil?"

I tried to remember the age at which I had learned the word "utensil." Ten?

While this woman was discussing a proper table setting, one of the girls decided to relax by changing her hairstyle.

"Allison, we're not going to pull out our ponytails, are we?"

Children generally do not learn rhetorical questions until they are two. Moreover, this question was particularly hard for Allison: she hadn't known what a horse was, so a ponytail was postgraduate work. Fortunately, because the question was rhetorical, Allison needed no comprehension of the words. She didn't know if *we* were going to pull out *our* ponytails, but *she* certainly was.

The boy in the teacher's lap was now massaging one of her breasts. When I myself had been a student, I had tried to do fieldwork in this exercise, though more in college than in nursery school. This, however, was the new accelerated age and I wondered if the teacher was going to see the boy's right hand not as a feckless feel but rather as an early lesson in human reproduction.

While I was wondering, she was suddenly distracted because one of the students had broken free and escaped into a plastic gym set.

"Colin, is *this* the time to climb?" she called to him.

Although giving no answer, Colin must have been thinking: No, New Year's Eve is the time. Why do you think I'm over here, lady? To *paint* the thing?

"Colin, after you've come down from the climber and rejoined all your friends, do you want to get another book from that little white case?"

These were the most difficult instructions the boy had received in his twelve months, for he didn't understand a single word: not "climber" or "book" or "little white case." He *might* have known his name was Frank, but there was a good chance he thought it was Morty.

As I watched him toddle away from the playground equipment, I was struck by a moment of truth: Americans have demonized childhood play. It was hardly as deathless a thought as *Give me liberty or give me death*, words these kids might have been thinking, but it did capture what might have been the last grim burst of Puritan thought in America: Play has no value unless it teaches. Play is a waste of time unless it is self-improving. All play and no work makes Jack a waiting-list boy.

The cliché that "play is children's work" has been too easily forgotten. We are turning normal childish behavior into an illness, said Richard Rothstein in *The New York Times,* and nothing was more fit to print for a nation that *should* have been letting its smallest citizens throw food, dump blocks, and eat paper in merry nonmetaphysical ways.

The weight of solid professional opinion opposes formal instruction in any domain of infants and young children, said David Elkind. *They need a warm, supportive, and non-pressured environment.*

This school was two out of three: The teachers were certainly warm and supportive. If only they hadn't been trying to prepare the kids for the SATs.

Study of gifted and talented people who were successful adults, said Elkind, *gives no support to the idea that early formal instruction creates intellectual giftedness or creative talent.*

In other words, Einstein, Da Vinci, and Madame Curie might have thought that hippos were called utensils until they were seven.

The oppressive programming of kids does more than just end childhood a decade or two too soon; and it does more than just give a kid the chance to be a world-class neurotic. It also stifles creativity, which isn't measured by multiple choice. While trying to produce Mensa mites, push-parents can't schedule that sweet time-waster called imagining, for which there are no Cliffs Notes. Emily Dickinson never pulled an all-nighter to cram for flights of fancy and Robert Louis Stevenson's mother never had him tutored in dreaming of ships.

When I left the Brighter Baby Learning Center, I went to Professor Ruddy for another dose of perspective. After I had shown her the center's literature and described the Goldfish class, she said, "Kids of twelve months sitting at tables? The only way to do that is to *feed* them."

"Yes," I said, "*some* of the food was getting into the kids. But is anything besides their stomachs being enriched?"

"I'm afraid not. Those kids are being passive and that's less stimulating to brain growth than letting them crawl around and explore things."

"One of them did try to explore the teacher's breasts," I said. "It was a boy, so does that count as sex education?"

"Well, it counts as better than someone reading at a whole group," she said. "That kind of reader can't pick up and respond to any interest or initiative."

"Believe me, there was no interest. There *was* some initiative, mostly to escape. One of the boys came over to me, probably thinking I could get him out."

"Only one-to-one reading could benefit that age. Seeing if the child leans toward a picture or makes some kind of sound. . . . Those kids would be just as unresponsive to a TV in front of the classroom. And a TV might be better because of the sound and music."

"If they were watching TV, the school could call it '*the development of consumer mentality.*'"

"Yes, how these places love to think that grand abstract things are going on! That booklet says, *When children put on dress clothes, they are learning small muscle skills.* No, they are learning to *pretend,* which happens to be much better. Of course, it's *play*. The thing is, young children learn and develop through play. And now we don't value it anymore."

"It seems as though we've gone back to Salem."

"Yes, play has become an inappropriate activity."

"Attending a class at twelve months seems like the most inappropriate activity. But it *is* a nice little snack bar."

"You know," said Professor Ruddy, "there's a pediatrician, Maria Escolar, who says that solo play for a one-year-old leads to all the good things: independence, self-confidence, creativity, and even *language* skills. She says you see fifteen-month-old kids jabbering to themselves as they play alone and that's basic to developing linguistic skill."

I had arrived at a towering truth: For a child of twelve to twenty months, the ideal student-teacher ratio was one-to-none.

My mention of Salem to Professor Ruddy started me wondering about early childhood three centuries before America had embraced misdirected education. The disapproval of children acting like children had begun in that long-ago time when fun was a four-letter word. Seventeenth-century Salem was the pilot project for the Better Baby Institute, the Bright Start Learning Centers, and every card-carrying mother who felt guilty whenever her child was childish, who felt desperation whenever her child toddled down a dead end called play.

Suddenly I could see the pure early-American source of it all: a Creepy Calvinists class in a preparatory school for going to hell. Three-year-olds Tabitha, Absolute, Relative,

Driven Snow, Increase, Decrease, Priscilla, Cotton, Rayon, and John are seated in a circle, all dressed in black, even though school uniforms are not mandatory.

"Good morning, worms," says the teacher, who then sounds a note on a flute and sings:

> *The itsy-bitsy spider*
> *Is you and everyone*
> *Who doesn't know*
> *The wickedness of fun.*

"And now for show-and-tell," she says. "Show us your friend and tell us why you are turning him or her in. Yes, Absolute."

"I saw Increase *playing!*" says Absolute.

"I *never* play, you Satanic simpleton!" says Increase. "I don't even know what play *is*."

"You were rolling a hoop across the green."

"That wasn't *play*, you moron. That was the development of my deltoid function, the refinement of my hand-eye coordination, *and* my comprehension of history as a constantly circular repetition, a wheel of hauntingly similar events, an endlessly echoing cycle."

"Oh," says Absolute. "I thought you were rolling a hoop."

11

Not Boola Boola but Buddha Buddha

For children too young to take starter Prozac or My Very First Valium, there is now a kind of itsy-bitsy rehab called Yippee Yoga just outside Boston in Cambridge. The inevitable response to the growing frenzy of push-parenting, Yippee Yoga claims to soothe the wee budding neurotics for whom the fast track has been the road to stress. The youngest student is two years old, not visibly tense, but with the promise of becoming a nervous wreck.

"Introducing these children to yoga calms them down and lets them reconnect to their inner rhythm," said Rosemary Simms, a former preschool teacher who is the head of Yippee Yoga. "Children's yoga goes back to prenatal patterns in the womb. The message is to come back to a wholeness that connects to one's organs and lets the children be where they already are."

Be where they already are?

I had hit the bottom of the rabbit hole: This woman made Glenn Doman, Don Campbell, and Carista Luminare-Rosen sound rational. Of course, I had to concede that my Western mind couldn't find the sense in such ethereal Zen insights as returning to a place while still remaining where you already were.

I knew where *I* already was: in a place that defied even Einsteinian understanding: To connect your organs with a wholeness while embracing prenatal patterns *post*natally. Was this some reincarnation of early Asian acrobatics? Was it a mystical blending of forehand and afterbirth? Was it a return to the womb through Nepal?

Once a week for an hour at the Cambridge studio of Rosemary Simms, for a fee of $20 an hour, children escaped from the pressures of saturated schedules by trying to become Buddha's boys and girls.

When I entered the studio's big room at three o'clock for the class, the scent of incense was in the air, giving the room the feeling of a Persian bazaar. Perhaps this was the ideal air for the decompression of kids in an *anti*structure. On soft mats arranged like the spokes of a wheel, Rosemary was placing bright scarves for ten kids, ages two to seven, who came in and began to both roll and squirm on the carpet as she said, "Do you want to take your socks off now?"

"No," said a boy of about four.

Gandhi would have liked his passive resistance.

Cheerfully rising above the rebuff, Rosemary sang the class's opening recitative:

> *Come and be nimble, come and be quick.*
> *Let's all be nimble, let's all be quick.*

I didn't think that agility and speed were essential to tranquillity, but I of course was a Type A nail biter, although I did like to take off my socks.

While Rosemary sang, every student sat on a mat except one boy, who lay on his back with a look of tranquil distress.

After Rosemary had sung more recitative, all the kids lay down and she said, "Now imagine snowflakes melting in the sun. . . . As the sun shines down on what used to be a big mountain of snow, a beautiful garden begins to emerge where the children play."

And then she wafted a silk scarf over the face of each child while singing:

> *Good morning to you,*
> *Good morning to you.*
> *We're all in our places*
> *With sunshiny faces,*
> *Oh, this is the way*
> *To start a new day.*

She was singing "Good morning" in midafternoon, but it was morning in Katmandu and perhaps she was taking the children there, or perhaps to San Francisco. She was a transcendental Mister Rogers, who could have been singing:

> *It's such a good feeling to know you're alive,*
> *Especially if this is life number five.*
> *So you will wake up ready to say:*
> *Mommy, see me transmigrate today!*

I wondered how much of her performance was meaningless play and how much was Buddhism for babes. Was this the American form of a Romper Room in Rangoon? While I wondered, she chanted her way into a Disneyland full of talking animals and an articulate atmosphere:

"And then the blowing winds whispered to the flowers and grass and everyone rocked in the warm spring sun and the shoots popped up. Wake up, wake up. Spring is coming."

Next Sunday was a return to Daylight Savings Time, but Rosemary was giving only timelessly rustic thoughts to the kids, who now crossed their legs and began to rock back and forth on their mats. Was this to be the new soft rock for stressed young America? It wasn't for one of the boys, who lay motionless on his face, either in enlightenment or in sleep.

Yoga involved the inscrutable and this class was inscrutable to me. As one ninth-century Chinese preschool teacher often asked, *What is the sound of one kid napping?*

"Let us now honor the sun with a spring flower dance," said Rosemary, who seemed to have danced out of

Woodstock. "Let us go into the forest and wake up all the animals."

One of the animals to awaken was the boy who'd been trying to get some sleep. Rosemary tapped him on the head, and then began moving from child to child, tapping each on the head with a stuffed bluebird. This baptism by bluebird energized a couple of the worshipers, who began to toss other stuffed animals around the room. It looked like normal childish behavior to me; but, once again, I probably couldn't divine the higher meaning of flying turtles and ducks.

No matter what the children did, Rosemary was so rampantly happy that I worried about her mind, which was in either a state of grace or collapse; her smile was so constant that the Maharishi might have wanted to pop her one. The boy who'd been praying independently now smiled at me and waved, giving me what felt like a blessing from another world. Meanwhile, Rosemary led everyone else in a walk around the room to find ducks that were sleeping in the mud.

At this point, the congregation had two new dropouts: a golden-haired girl of about four and a boy about five with thick brown curls, both of whom decided that they didn't give a damn about ducks that were sleeping in the mud, or even ones served with glaze. While Rosemary led the others to the mud, these two played with each other in dry duckless contentment.

"And a beautiful shoot popped out of the earth," said Rosemary, "and said, 'Good morning, dear earth. Good morning, dear sun. Good morning to you and good morning to me.'"

Was this an ancient Druid rite? No, it was a contemporary steal from *Goodnight Moon.*

And suddenly, just after Rosemary had been a slithering snake that honored the sun with a dance, my own burst of insight came when she sang:

> *Row, row, row your boat*
> *Gently down the stream.*
> *Merrily, merrily, merrily, merrily,*
> *Life is but a dream.*

Once again, I was aware of what I had learned long ago, both from my own life and from Creepy Crawlers: life is a dream. And an even grander insight was my awareness of another cosmic truth I had always known: that no matter how dreamy or dreary life might be, absolutely *nothing* in it was sweeter than seeing small children just being children, something they knew how to do with no operator's manual being read to them by adults. Acting like children was simply a state of grace into which children were born. I wondered why so many adults were now trying to fix what not only wasn't broken but was a time of blessedness.

After having the kids do more rocking, Rosemary sang a song about bees, told the kids to stand on one leg while buzzing, and then flitted around the room to touch a bee puppet to each student's head. Three of the boys decided that this was an elective and they buzzlessly sat down.

Moments later, Rosemary told all the others to lie down and look at the lovely sun overhead. For the three, however, it was raining, and the smallest one jumped up and took cover in a corner of the room. In Princeton, Philadelphia, and now Cambridge, I had seen such breakaways from structure by young children, even when the structure was the unbroken cheerfulness of a New England flower child.

"And while they rested," said Rosemary, "a beautiful baby cloud came over them, a special cloud that awakened them from their dreams. Can you see it? Would you like to talk to it?"

"No," said the boy who still was honoring Gandhi.

"Very well, then, if you don't want to, just say, 'No, thank you, baby cloud,' and then it won't be there for you."

From time to time, I had talked to the sky and to traffic, too; I had once engaged in a lively exchange with a parking meter; but a higher plane of consciousness had never been my address. These kids, however, were being given the feeling that they were attuned to a cosmic cuteness, that the heart of yoga was Yogi Bear. I would have been Scrooge to fault that feeling, for perhaps seeing the world as a cartoon full of talking gardens and zoos would one day keep the kids from throwing blunt objects at their mothers, or setting fire to their schools, or going online to try to siphon money from Chase.

"We love you, sun, and we thank you," said Rosemary, leaving me even more confused about the worship going on here. She sounded like a naturalized Inca who had spent her junior year in Tibet.

After being polite to the climate, the kids made a big circle around a candle that Rosemary lit while saying, "Just like the sun, this is the light that shines in our hearts." The occult symbolism was thickening for Rosemary's babies.

"Thank you, candle," she said, and then she blew it out and gave sugar wafers to all of them.

"You may put these in your mouths," she said.

Was this just snack time, or was it a kind of chewy communion?

Turning from the smoking candle, she picked up a bell and gave it to one of the children, who began to pass it around the circle to the others.

"Now close your eyes and make a bell ring inside your head," she said. "Can you hear it? . . . Listen to the bell. . . *Oom . . . oom . . . oom.*"

The kids were moving even deeper into what I presumed was the mysticism of Zen, and this might have been the moment when they began falling off the fast track to Yale. The SATs were not for kids who were dingy enough to think that a bell went *oom.*

"*Shanti, shanti, shanti, oom, oom, oom,*" said Rosemary. "Shanti means peace. It's a very old word that comes from the land where yoga comes from. Does anyone know what that land is?"

"Boston," said one of the boys.

"That's *almost* right," she said.

I had never seen such positive thinking.

"Brookline," said one of the girls.

"That's *very* close. It's *India*. You certainly know your geography."

The way that geography was now being taught in American schools, Brookline could have been the capital of India to kids three times the age of Ned; but the whole point of Yippee Yoga was to free these kids from the pressure to know anything, to let them embrace a higher wisdom and put Calcutta on I-95.

"And now," said Rosemary, "does anyone want to share something about the earth with us today? Maxwell?"

"I went to Toys ' Я ' Us," said Maxwell.

"Yes, Toys ' Я ' Us is part of the earth."

"It's in Newton."

"It's almost Passover," said Clifford.

"My snail died," said Heather.

"This is my yoga ball," said Clifford, holding up an invisible one.

I didn't know what the hell anyone was talking about, but perhaps nonsequiturs were the road to enlightenment—if not for me, then for the kids. Perhaps this was the only way to respond to the escalating absurdity of modern life.

"Let us now greet the earth," said Rosemary. "Good morning, dear earth. Good morning, dear sun. Good morning, dear cat. Good morning, dear dog. Good morning to you and good morning to me."

She was doing a Moony *Goodnight Moon*, her version of the world's most enchanting children's story, and her version was making ten children smile.

"And the dog went . . ."

"Bow wow," said the kids.

"And the cat went . . ."

"Mew, mew."

"And the swan went . . ."

"Mew, mew."

It was a swan that did cat imitations; but the surrealism of this world was more appealing than the surrealism of the one in which the sun was greeted not with good morning but with the Gettysburg Address, the world in which toddlers were turned into calculators, cornflakes were visual aids, fetuses were captive audiences, and America was crawling with diapered da Vincis.

In the last twenty minutes of the class, the kids did rocking, rolling, marching, deep breathing, animal sounds, and hopping like frogs. One of the frogs, who seemed about three, hopped over to me.

"*Shanti*," I said, and he laughed.

"*Shanti* back," he said.

"*Shanti oom*," I said, and he laughed again. He was probably Reformed Buddhist. "Do you like yoga, Mr. Frog?"

"Yes," he replied.

"Why do you like it?"

"I like it because I like it," he said, one of ten tiny Zen masters in a nursery school full of insense and noncense.

After the class had ended and mothers were bringing the kids back to earth, Rosemary talked to me about what she had done, no doubt suspecting that I hadn't understood it.

"I try to remove the tension from them," she said.

"Can a two-year-old really *have* tension?" I said. "Isn't that something we teach him when he's a little older?"

"No," she said, "some of them already are starting to have lower back problems."

"You can barely *find* their lower backs."

"You know, children are really just little adults."

"A lot of the country is thinking that way. Childhood is being reduced to a couple of years—and sometimes less."

"Well, we do have to shape the children early."

"Some of the shaping I've seen is like Silly Putty. But you *are* very gentle here."

"Yes, I try to relax the children and to find for them a place between their centers and their movements. I'm exploring their connections to their spines."

"Those connections are worth exploring? And how can you do it without surgery?"

She laughed. "You really don't understand yoga, do you?"

"Well, I didn't when I came in, and now I understand a little less."

"It's simple. I try to let each child find his prevertebrate self."

Rosemary's answer to push-parenting was to let the children ask themselves if they used to be jellyfish, the only people in America involved with both Darwin and stuffed animals. She was going the other way from Glenn Doman, who wanted children to find their postreptilian selves. He had felt that the smallest ones developed fastest when they were crawling and shedding their old ideas for the ones he was selling for only $144 UPS second-day delivery.

Leaving Rosemary's studio for the unscented world, I suddenly wanted to cry out, Can't all of you just leave them alone? Can't you stop probing, prodding, and programming them? Give them toys and hugs and DPT shots, but in the name of humanity stop trying to *redesign* them? Prenatal U, Better Baby, Creepy Crawlers, Bright Start Child, Fun for None, Reconstructed Toddler, Postnatal Upgrade—*time out!* Can't you recognize a masterpiece of nature when you see one? American kids are so damn lucky to live in a land where kids can *enjoy* a childhood instead of the joy of making underwear for twelve cents an hour. No *wonder* your intelligence is being replaced by the artificial kind!

I thought of J. D. Salinger's quotation of the ancient Chinese line: *A child is a guest in the house, to be loved and respected—never possessed, since he belongs to God.* Well, God was now Vince Lombardi.

Walking back toward Boston, I thought about John and Sam Adams and the men with whom they had invented a wondrous country that now was losing its way in the nursery. How had the Adams boys, Jefferson, Franklin, Hamilton, Madison, and Washington, become such magnificent adults after having had no early acceleration? Not one of them as a toddler had ever been shown two cards with pictures of monarchs and asked, "Which king is the idiot?"

12

Pop Goes the Poppa

"Harry, goddamnit, throw *strikes!*"

It was heartfelt fatherly guidance for a nine-year-old pitcher from the man who was living through him at what was supposed to be a game. In a time when millions of American parents were having out-of-body experiences with their children, this particular father was exploring new levels of child possession. It was traditional for a Little League father to wait at least a couple of innings before starting to threaten his son, but Harry's father saw his other self walk the leadoff hitter and he had no choice: he activated the control tower at once.

I wasn't seeing toddlers under gentle female pressure now: I was seeing preteens whose fathers had abandoned all pretense of having their own lives, hoping to be reincarnated as their uniformed children. A spectator at the ballfield on this bright summer day could have known that Harry and his father were related because they both had red hair, similar features, and were both about five feet tall, although Harry didn't comb his hair from back to front.

A chubby boy with a cherubic face, Harry was pitching for the Beavers against the Reds in the top of the first inning of a seven-inning hardball game that should have been evoking Norman Rockwell and not Norman Bates. Some parents were still arriving and just settling in for an afternoon of driving their children crazy.

It was hard to analyze Harry's performance at this point because he had faced only the leadoff man and had walked him, possibly because the leadoff man was less than four feet tall and reminded me of a midget who once had pinch-hit for the St. Louis Browns. Harry's father, however, no giant of a man himself in any way, was taking no chance that he might have to tell his fellow car salesmen on Monday that the Beavers had lost, so he was offering some early suggestions.

"Harry, goddamnit, start *pitching!*"

This advice perhaps was superfluous: Harry wasn't serving or teeing off; pitching was what he must have been doing.

"Look where you're throwing the *goddamn ball!*"

Another unnecessary tip: Harry *was* looking in that direction—it wouldn't have made sense to be facing the outfield—but now he had a runner on first and was facing another batter of inconsequential height, to whom his first two pitches were balls.

"What the hell are you *doing? Jesus,* throw *strikes!*"

Harry probably wished that Jesus were pitching instead of him. It was, however, his good luck that the batter had a void in competence that included both judgment and coordination: Harry continued to throw what would have been balls, but the hitter—hardly the proper word—turned three of them into strikes, as did the two hitters after him. Along with paternal intervention, there was also the divine variety that had enabled Harry to strike out the side.

Striking out the side would have pleased a father whose mind was hinged, but Harry's father was pushing push-parenting to new heights, which were also new depths. When Harry left the mound for the Beavers' turn at bat, his father met him at the foul line and began a private clinic in how to pitch: He took Harry's arm and began bringing it down in what was either a pitcher's motion or the motion for drying his hand. Undoubtedly an athletic failure in college and in postgraduate life as well, Harry's father looked like a man with a command of playing little more than lotto.

"You bring your wrist down like *this*," he said as other parents began shouting pleas, corrections, and commands to their smaller selves. "You're releasing the ball too *soon*. How many times do I hafta *tell* you that? You're a *Beaver*. So *give* a damn!"

They were words from a squirrel to a child who may have been wishing he were conferring with a soccer mom at this baseball game. In spite of the lunatic loose on the field, I was delighted to see small children playing America's greatest game instead of the lesser one that had grown even more popular than dieting or tax evasion. In this country, where boys like me had gone to sleep clutching not stuffed animals but hardballs, softballs, and spaldeens, too many fields of dreams were now sunny memorial parks for soccer, the great Albanian game. Baseball had lost far too many kids to soccer, and the reason was clear: hitting a baseball is the hardest thing in all sport to do. With a soccer ball, every kid is Ted Williams.

And now the Beavers were trying to execute sport's hardest maneuver, while Harry escaped from his private lesson to the on-deck circle. On the first pitch, the leadoff man tried to bunt, spinning around and holding his bat as if he were waterskiing. He missed the ball by just a couple of feet, and his father cried, "Sammy, you got *eyes?*"

Unfortunately, Sammy also had ears, and they were hearing not only his father's anatomical question but also denials of his existence from people outside his family:

"*No* batter! *No* batter! He's *nobody!* He's *nuthin'!*" came the cries, and they came from adults, or people who resembled adults. When I had played stickball, the good-natured heckling, such as "Your mother does it for sailors!" came only from the boys in the game; but now that the boys were parental puppets, their fathers and mothers, too, were enjoying an afternoon of child abuse with such implied messages as, You're not out there to have *fun!* Get a hit or you're out of the will! and How'd you like to find another place to sleep!

With his confidence at zero, the batter struck out, probably wondering if he would be put up for adoption, and

Harry came to the plate. At once his father shouted with new acumen: "Harry, your bat is to *hit* the damn ball!"

On the first pitch Harry swung and accidentally hit a ground ball that the pitcher played with for a while and then threw to first as Harry was about to arrive. It looked like a tie to me, but not to the umpire, who threw up his thumb, giving Harry's father renewed participation in the game.

"Are you out of your goddamn *mind?*" he cried as he ran to the umpire, who was ready to put the same question to him. "Don't you see *anything?*"

"*Out,*" said the umpire.

"He was *safe,* you moron!"

"Get off the field," said the umpire.

"*You're* the one who should get off the field!"

For the next thirty seconds Harry's father screamed abuse that he had been saving for Harry. The man was showing why America had reached a point where becoming a parent should have required a license after a mental examination.

A few days before this game, the *New York Times* had said, *From hockey arenas in Maine to soccer fields in New Mexico, parents are yelling and jeering—even spitting and brawling—as never before.* People like Harry's father were all the rage.

The previous week at the soccer game of a neighbor's child, I had seen a referee banish a father who had called him a cretin. Although it was unfortunate for the kids to see a father with the self-control of Donald Duck, at least "cretin" *was* a good word to learn; it might appear on the SAT.

During this particular display of recreation rage, there was no one to banish Harry's father, who reminded me of the Florida coach who had made a point to one of his boys by breaking both his arms. Had Harry's father done the same, he would have written on one of the boy's casts: *Only a wimp takes refuge in orthopedics! Get back in the game!*

At last, Harry's father fell silent, to ponder new obscenities, and the next batter came up and hit the ball through a hole created when the first baseman was called into conference by *his* father. This play seemed to unsettle the Reds' pitcher, who then gave up two runs. Both of them, however, were unearned, caused by fielders' difficulty in locating and taking possession of balls.

When Harry returned to the mound in the top of the second with a two-run lead, logic would have said that his father would become a silent spectator; but logic has no place in Little League play today. Eager for Harry not just to win but to pitch a shutout as well, the man now began to call the pitches for his son to throw. The batters, of course, also heard these suggestions, but gained no advantage, because Harry had not the slightest idea how any of the pitches should have been thrown. He was deeply gratified every time the ball went in the general direction of home plate.

"Harry, now the *curve!*" cried his father. "The *curve!*"

Perhaps somewhere in America or Taiwan was a nine-year-old who could throw a curve, but Harry wasn't that boy.

After throwing a pitch that wasn't a curve or anything else, Harry heard, "Okay, now the *change-up!*"

This pitch Harry could throw by taking something off his nothing ball so that it moved even slower, almost defying a law of physics. Unfortunately, the first time Harry threw it, the batter hit the ball to the shortstop and was safe on a fielder's choice: the fielder chose not to throw to first, perhaps holding the ball to keep the batter from taking an extra base.

Enraged that Harry had lost his no-hitter, his father cried, "What the hell are you guys doin' out there, playin' games? Okay, Harry, stick the next one in his ear!"

In response to this suggestion to crack his son's skull, the batter's father cried, "Let the bad ones go, Manny, and cream a good one!"

In his entire Little League career, Manny had been unable to cream or even milk a good one; but Harry now decided to be a good son and see if, in a sporting way, he could give the boy a little concussion: he threw the next pitch at Manny's head. It was, however, Manny's good luck that Harry's pitches were always surprises to Harry: the next one came straight across the plate, and Manny hit it as if a voice from Fatima had guided his bat.

The ball rolled straight to the shortstop, a ball that cried double play; but the shortstop was able to miss both outs because of a flaw in his fielding: he was afraid of ground balls. He got no error on the play; with balletic rather than baseball grace, he had moved away from the ball to let it go cleanly through.

"Douglas, get that ball!" his father suggested.

Knowing where his bread was buttered, Douglas moved smartly after the ball. It is uncommon in baseball for the shortstop to run out to straightaway left field. In fifty years of watching baseball, I had never seen it happen; but Douglas was wise to take a trip out there because the left fielder had been blowing bubbles, as well as the play; he seemed to have been unaware that the ball was in his neighborhood.

As both runners rounded the bases, Douglas and the left fielder met at the ball, and a moment later the center fielder joined them. Beaver fans had the comfort of knowing that this play was well covered.

"Lemme throw it!" Douglas cried.

"No lem*me!*" the center fielder said.

"It's *my position!*" said the left fielder, not without logic.

"Fuck you!" said Douglas to either one or both of his teammates; I couldn't tell if he was being selective or all-inclusive.

By the time the ball reached the cutoff man, who happened to be the right fielder, the Reds had two runs, the game was tied, and Harry's father was cultivating a stroke. Even in the depths of his lunacy, he couldn't blame Harry for having thrown what should have been a double-play ball; but he *was* able to blame Harry for not backing up the play at the plate, even though there was no play at the plate because the ball had stayed pretty much in the outfield.

And now Harry's father saw a sight that would have driven him mad had he not been there already: the Beavers' manager brought in a new pitcher. Running to the manager, Harry's father cried, "Why you taking him out? He's pitching great!"

"I want to give *all* the boys a chance to play," said the manager, displaying ill-advised maturity.

"Don't you want to *win?*" screamed Harry's father.

Silently, the manager looked at him as if he needed an exorcist.

The president of Sarah Lawrence College had recently said, "Do we really want to teach our children that life is all about beating the competition?"

Had he heard these words, Harry's father, now drowning in despair, would have said, Those Sarah Lawrence teams must really suck.

As the Beavers' new pitcher warmed up, his father stood near first base, smiling with pride while pounding his right fist into his open left hand.

"Okay, Danny," he called to the boy, "it's murder time. Let's *kill* these guys!"

Unable to keep listening to the snapping of minds, I strolled away from the field, turned my face to the sun, and closed my eyes. And then I let myself drift back to the days before fathers of young players had joined the criminally insane . . .

13

The Way We Were

The president of Sarah Lawrence College would have liked seeing my youngest daughter, Lori, at the age of Harry's son, in the last days when kids played for themselves and not the glory of pathological parents. In that quaint time, Lori was in a third-grade kickball game that had the sporting intensity of a Parisian picnic. Lori's gym teacher had said, "Don't worry about the score, just have fun," words revealing that America was a foreign country for her.

By the third week of the kickball season, Lori had a batting average of about .700, for she consistently kicked extra base hits through defenses of more than a dozen players. In those games, there was no such thing as a single in the hole for the hole contained five or six shortstops, none of whom could go to his left because another shortstop was blocking his way. However, even a version of baseball that looked like rush hour was a wondrous game to Lori.

As a kicker, she quickly developed the ability to guess right on every pitch, perhaps because every pitch was a straight roller down the middle, a hanging beachball. Every pitch was a mistake, although it *was* hard for a pitcher to do much with a kickball but roll a fat one or deflate it. Nevertheless, even though the average fielder was skilled at bouncing the ball off the cutoff man, Lori's first inside-the-park home run was so intoxicating that she ran home from school almost as fast to share it with me.

She had found a pitch that was just her shoe size and driven it into a crowd of center fielders. As she was dashing for third, one of the fielders played the carom off a friend and tried to hit her with the ball, a throw that would have tested Willie Mays, but she pirouetted away, and then she eluded another fielder, who chased her home with the ball.

"It was so great, Daddy!" she said. "They threw it at me and they chased me with it, but I got all the way to home base!"

"Home *plate*," I said. "Well, honey, I'm really proud of you. Tell me: Do they ever try *tagging* people at those bases?"

"Why would they do *that?*"

"It's a crazy way baseball is played sometimes."

"Daddy, I *love* baseball."

"And you'll love it even more when you play it."

The following year, when she was ten, Lori learned what loving baseball could be.

Because I had passed some of the happiest days of my boyhood at a ballpark with my father, I used to dream of recapturing such days with my own son. My first child, however, was a girl, who somehow grew to like lacrosse, a sensible sport if her father had been a Chippewa and could have taken her out to the old stick game.

My second child was also a girl, who somehow grew to like field hockey, and once said to me, "Baseball is boring," voicing the equivalent of a belch in St. Patrick's Cathedral.

And then came Lori and I waited gloomily for this third daughter also to be blind to baseball and perhaps turn to bullfighting and keep up with the scores from Tijuana.

Just after her tenth birthday, however, my friend Alan took Lori and me to Shea Stadium to see a Mets-Cardinals game. As he led us into the park, I felt the jolt of pleasure that only the first sight of baseball grass can bring to a man over fifty. I bought a program, a hot dog, and a Mets cap for Lori as if I were saving her soul.

When the game began, Lori joined the crowd in crying Mooo-kie! Mooo-kie! Mooo-kie!" It was a sound that Margaret Mead might have heard in Samoa, but this tribe was using it to greet a lithe and blithe center fielder who at once enchanted my little girl.

On that intoxicating day, when Lori fell in love with the Mets, when she added her voice to the thousands who sang "Take Me Out to the Ball Game" as if it were the national anthem, I owed $5,000 to the Internal Revenue Service and my dentist had been discussing canals with the glee of Teddy Roosevelt in Panama; but I knew that I was safe, that nothing bad could happen to a man at a baseball game when beside him a daughter with mustard-stained lips was demanding, "Let's go, Mets!"

The next night at dinner Lori said, "Gary Carter is really in a clump."

"That's *slump*, honey," I replied.

"A clump is worse than a slump," she said.

What a splendid new word, one that not even Red Barber or Beanie might have coined! Not only was my daughter in love with the world's greatest game but she also was enriching its language; no mere *son* could have done any better! I felt as elated as if Lori had just won a spelling bee. And she *could* have won a spelling bee, for she knew that there were three *o*'s in Mooo-kie. It was, however, poor preparation for the SATs.

A few Sundays later, we returned to Shea, where Lori now knew that three-and-one was a hitter's pitch, that Roger McDowell blew wonderful bubbles, that the Cardinals had no class, and that a high five was not a basketball team on cocaine.

As we stood in one of the boxes beside the Mets' dugout to watch batting practice, one of the Cardinals, Andy Van Slyke, caught sight of Lori's fetching face beneath her Mets cap and came over with a ball for her.

"Here, cutie," he said. "For you."

She thanked him and clutched the ball as if holding her firstborn, and I silently apologized to the Cardinals for having hoped they would all come down with scurvy. It was the

kind of wish that American fathers would soon be having
for boys foul enough to be playing against their sons.

* * *

Two years later, when Lori was twelve and American children were in the last days of playing sports for just their
own enjoyment, I helped her leave kickball behind and
learn how to play The Game, in which she wanted to be
the first female second baseman in the major leagues. And
not for a moment did I want her to be an extension of me.
No father would have wanted to extend mediocrity.

"Stop throwing sidearm," I told her at an empty diamond
on a day in late June, "except on a bunt; you'll make too
many bad throws to first."

"You think I have a good arm?" she said.

"You do."

"Then say so. Say 'Good arm, good arm.'"

"Okay. Good arm, good arm. Big head, big head."

"How many positions do you think I could play?"

"At once?"

"*Daddy!*"

"Let's just work on second. *I* never got that one right. I
kept wanting to play it with a spaldeen; I was afraid of
ground balls."

"You were *afraid* of ground balls?

"Just the ones coming at me. Okay, here they come: some
line drives first. . . . Two hands—and watch the ball all the
way. Never look at the runners or anything else, . . . *That's*
it; *good* . . . no, turn your mitt *up* for those. Keep it facing

up and it won't bounce out . . . a high one now, the kind my father used to throw me."

"Was baseball the same back then?"

"When General Grant was commissioner? No, we played it with canoe paddles and tangerines."

"*Daddy!*"

"Yes, the same. Except for AstroTurf and the DH. And the splitter and batting gloves. And $10 million for a .250 hitter."

"*I* can hit .250."

"Girls may have to hit .350."

"*That* stinks."

"Well, no daughter of mine is *allowed* to hit below that . . . okay, some pop-ups now."

Circling under a fly ball, she caught it with a one-handed swat that made me sink with a sense of passing time.

"More of those," she said.

"But don't *swat* them. You're not catching flies, you're . . . catching flies. Use *two* hands."

"Everybody uses one hand. Two hands I'll look goofy."

"Like DiMaggio."

"*He* used two?"

"Every time."

"Because one-handed wasn't invented yet."

"I knew there was a reason. Okay, some grounders."

"I'm really great on those!"

"Keep your head down and your eye on the ball. And stay in front of it."

All the things I never did.

"Daddy, don't you think I know anything? This is *my game*."

When she had finished the fielding practice, she took some swings at pitches from me.

"Stop uppercutting," I said with the wisdom of someone whose batting weakness had been anything thrown by a pitcher. "Swing straight through."

"I like 'em low," she said.

"Fine. You'll say that in a note to the pitcher."

A few minutes later she belted a drive to right center that left me elated.

"Triple!" she cried.

"Double. Willie's out there."

"He's about *fifty* now."

"He still got to it."

"You think I'll hit one like that in the game?"

"It's very possible. You're swinging well now. Just relax and concentrate."

"But you can't do *both*. Did *you* do both?"

"Usually neither."

One afternoon the following week, I was in the stands at Lori's day camp for her first competitive game of softball. In her first at bat, with her bat straight up like Musial's and Freddie's, she did a quick twist of her hips before hitting a drive past the shortstop and making it to second. As she ran, her ponytail was flapping under her Mets cap and I felt as though I had been swigging champagne.

Unfortunately, the second baseman, a girl who was a harbinger of the Age of Adult Athletic Abuse, told Lori she had looked like a dork by putting her hips in action at bat. When Lori came off the field between innings, she told me the story with tears in her eyes.

"Forget her; she's stupid," I said. "What a great *hit* you got!"

"If she calls me a dork again," she said, "I'm going to punch her. I may punch her anyway."

"If you want to punch, play hockey. Look, you're going to be the female Jackie Robinson, right?"

"Right."

"Then you're going to have to take it. You know what they called Jackie when he first came up?"

"A bastard?"

"His *friends* called him that. But the others . . . "

"What?"

"You're too young to hear it. Now, just keep that nice level swing and *meet* the ball. Don't try to kill it like the other kids."

"Thanks, Dad. You're sweet."

"Never let anyone hear you saying that to your coach."

Had Lori's encounter with that gracious second baseman happened today, the second baseman's father would have come to me and said, "Your daughter is the sappy one who was *crying*? The game is maybe the wrong time of the month for her?"

"No," I would have replied, "she just turned twelve, but she's a *young* twelve. I know she *should've* hit puberty a few years ago, but—"

"And I suppose you think she's cute with that goddamn ponytail?"

"Well, I do find a certain charm in—"

"Ponytails are for horses' asses."

"You left yours at home?"

"Hey, you want me to rearrange your face? I've fixed a few in this league already, and they weren't all umpires. Buddy, you got any *other* children in play?"

"Yes, two other daughters, but they . . . well, they play all their games just for fun."

And then, with soulful disgust, he would say, "This country today . . . I don't know why North Korea hasn't attacked us already."

14

Driving Miss Hazy

And now I must make another confession: Looking at the spread of push-parenting, I realize that I was part of its early development. But I have two excuses, neither of which can bear too much analysis. First, I have never found anything in life better than being a father; second, I have been unemployed since the Cuban Missile Crisis. I did have a job for a couple of months in the fall of 1962, but I didn't like it and haven't wanted to just jump into another. I don't mean to boast, but I am very selective.

However, in the world of push-parenting, I never *pushed* but rather pressed the pedal in my years of driving daughters. And I see now that I was a capless chauffeur in a preview of the overdrive to come. In fact, *Driving Miss Daisy* was a routine run when compared to my years of what might have been called Downhill Effacer.

As Tolstoy said when he told his five daughters to hop into the sled, happy families are all alike in towns with no public transportation. My own daughters often used their bikes to go to school, stores, and the homes of friends, but they hailed my cab whenever it was dark or ten degrees, or whenever it was sunny and sixty. Those were not the days of chauffeuring the overscheduled but of just lending a hand to the stranded.

In that transitional time, my home office became a taxi stand where the telephone frequently rang to bring me the words "Dad, I need a pickup."

"Have you tried Ovaltine?" I once replied to one of my three.

"Dad, this is *serious*."

"Okay, you're talking to the dispatcher."

"Make it the flagpole at three, okay?"

"Will you have any baggage today?"

"Just my backpack."

Those were still the days when a student's backpack was carry-on luggage, before students began pulling their books on rolling carryalls like flight attendants. Whenever I see an aspiring Superkid today, I want to say, *Are you checking that on through to homeroom?*

How quietly charming those early days of transportation seem in this age of NASCAR moms. I remember one afternoon when I reached the flagpole of the high school at three o'clock to find my thirteen-year-old daughter, Lynn, with two of her friends; and in that bygone time, not one of the girls was wearing a nose ring or was visibly pregnant.

"Dad," said Lynn, "can we drop Debbie and Kelly off at their houses?"

"Of course," I said with a smile, relieved that I wasn't being asked to drop off their dry cleaning too.

I had no second smile, however, when I learned that Debbie and Kelly lived at opposite ends of town and should have been taking separate cabs.

"Debbie is Lincoln Lane and Kelly is Clearview," said Lynn as I softly brought up the overture to *Don Giovanni* on the radio. "Dad, *please!* We want *music!*"

In those days the Mozart Effect was indigestion; and so Lynn punched a button that filled the car with the kind of sounds that must have been heard at the fall of Khartoum. High school students today know nothing about the fall of Khartoum, although many embryos may be learning it.

After a few minutes of driving I said, "Anything happen at school today?"

"Not really," said Lynn in a voice that reminded me I had broken the parent-passenger relationship that is supposed to exist in a family cab: the parent must be visible only to other drivers. I was, however, merely performing the time-less role of the father of a daughter: embarrassing her. Not *all* fathers, of course, embarrass their daughters: some mor-tify them.

"My dad had a fit last night," said Debbie, "just because I haven't practiced the piano for a month or two."

"Like, get off your *back*," said Kelly.

"Right. I mean, like you can't *skip* a month and a college will *know?* I mean, it's just too much *pressure.*"

How appealingly old-fashioned Debbie's rebellion against parental pressure now seems, in an age when free time and free will for children have been banished like polio. The only rebellion has been in Japan, mother lode of push-parenting, where from time to time a student jumps off a bridge, breaking his scholastic momentum, among other things.

"My dad keeps trying to make me stop saying 'like' so much," said Kelly. "Like, there's a grade in how good I speak?"

"My dad wants me to practice piano *and* not say 'like,'" said Lynn, as if her dad were in Kyoto. "I mean, one or the other."

Today, of course, practicing piano and speaking English are merely two of a dozen disciplines directed by parents who chauffeur not as silent soldiers but as Captain Blighs.

For the rest of the trip, I said nothing more, for already I had made the mistake of revealing that I existed. A chauffeur's window would have prevented this mistake, but I couldn't install one because Lynn always sat in front to tune the radio to the worst music since Nero's last gig.

When at last I had dropped off the other two scholars and brought Lynn home, I was free to go back to work for five or ten minutes, until it was time to drive her to a friend's house to do some homework. After this trip, I returned to the dispatcher's office and tried to remember what my other profession was.

"Do you think that Lynn would be upset if I got an unlisted number and didn't tell her for a year or two?" I said to Judy, who taught school so that she couldn't be called for rides.

"You really should try to stop being New Jersey Transit," said Judy. "You know, there's a girl down the street who rides her bike *everywhere*."

"Her parents are probably in prison."

That evening, in a moving display of character, Lynn requested no rides during dinner. After dinner I drove her and three friends to a ballet class, where I decided to wait with a book, *Escape from Freedom*. In those early days of parental roadrunners, I constantly had to decide: did it make sense to drive home to relax for fifteen minutes or stay at the lesson and read or stay at the lesson and polish the car? Today's chauffeur would stay and rough out an admissions essay that could be tailored to either Dalton or Duke.

On that particular evening I stayed and made shoptalk with the other chauffeurs, all of whom were female; and I saw the trend that would be producing a million internal combustion moms:

"Next Wednesday, Warren has soccer right before orthodontia," said one of them. "Do you think the dentist will be upset if the game goes into overtime?"

"Every day is like that for me," another mother said. "Just one overturned tractor-trailer and Sarah's whole day falls apart. We save a few seconds if she changes in the car, but she's getting self-conscious about taking off her clothes on Route 1."

"*I* used to take off my clothes in the car," said the first.

"We *all* did. It was a more relaxed time."

*   *   *

The following morning at breakfast Judy courageously said to Lynn, "Honey, Daddy and I would like you to ride your bike to school today and then to choir practice after."

With a stricken look Lynn replied, "Is something wrong with the *car*? Wrong with *Dad*?"

She had the correct order for concern.

"No, but it would be good for you," said Judy. "And Daddy could discover how it feels to spend a whole day at his job."

"Dad got a *job*? I thought he *writes*."

And so my daughter went to her bike and I looked forward to turning the dispatcher's office into my alternate one.

Twenty minutes later the phone rang.

"Dad, I'm really sorry to bother you," said a familiar voice, "but I left my algebra book in the kitchen."

"Could I FedEx it to you?" I said.

"Dad, this is *serious*. Could you bring it to the flagpole at ten?"

"Will I be returning empty, or is there someone who wants to drop out?"

At ten o'clock I drove a book to school, and it was my ideal passenger because it didn't mind my singing "Don't Fence Me In" and "Mairzy Doats." In ten years such books would be in hands much smaller than Lynn's. In ten years parents would be pushing for algebra to be taught in the second grade.

Harold, stop sucking your thumb and solve for X.

As I drove and sang, I was warmed by the thought that this was my last trip of the day, and the warmth of that thought lingered until the rain began to fall.

At three o'clock I was back at the school, where I picked up Lynn and put her bike in the trunk of the car. No longer was I just a chauffeur: I had become the Auto Train.

"Dad, we have a history assignment," she said as we rode home. "We have to pretend we're living in the eighteenth century."

"My favorite one," I said, picturing that lovely time before the birth of Henry Ford.

15

Miss Postpartum

The words "the end of civilization as we know it" are used too easily for such minor setbacks as the invention of voice mail and the birth of Richard Nixon. However, when I entered the ballroom of the Harrisburg Holiday Inn at nine o'clock one morning for the first event of the zero to five-year-olds in the annual Miss Crystal Dynasty Pageant, I felt that I was seeing not just the end of civilization as we know it but the final spasm of human life in Pennsylvania.

If God destroyed Sodom and Gomorrah merely for overzealous group sex, He might have wanted an encore when He saw obese young women whooping for one-, two-, and three-year-olds who were prancing flirtatiously with frozen smiles and loose hips. They were dears in the head-lights, these pageant contestants: their rich lip gloss reflected the video lights, their uneasy eyes were outlined by liner, and their blond upswept hair made them look like vest pocket Vanna Whites.

And Dante thought that *he* had seen the bottom.

I was now in a zone far below the ventriloquism of parents who were trying to turn preschoolers into Superkids for the Ivy League. These parents were trying to turn preschoolers into champions of a league called Glamour Doll USA, living through them not educationally but erotically. And now they were giving last-minute loving guidance to what were supposed to be children:

> For God's sake, don't let that tooth fall out!
> These aren't your lucky earrings!
> Look in their eyes and never stop smiling!
> The damn curlers came out too soon.
> What the hell are you crying about?
> Now can you remember that bad thing you did in Tennessee?
> Stop rubbing your blusher! Do you want to ruin your future?

Waiting for the first event to begin, I began leafing through my *Pride of Pageantry* magazine, the deviate's *Playboy*, and read about the only country in the world in which hundreds of thousands of people were possessed to eliminate childhood.

> BABY DIVISION: Under 3
> Tiny Baby Girls (2–17 months)
> Older Baby Girls (18–35 months)
> Tiny Baby Boys (2–17 months)
> Older Baby Boys (18–35 months)

GIRLS: From 3 to 25
Petite Girls (3–5)
Little Miss (6–9)
Junior Miss (10–12)
Teen Miss (13–17)
Miss (17–25)

MINI OPTIONALS
Prettiest Hair
Prettiest Eyes
Best Smile
Best Personality
Most Serious
Most Glamorous or Handsome
Cutest Kid

COVER WINNER GETS:
Hollywood Babe Outfit of Your Choice
Dyeable Satin Shoes or Pumps
Embroidered Garment Bag
Rhinestone Crown Pin

CENTERFOLD WINNER GETS:
Two Full Pages in the Magazine
Princess Acrylic Clear Shoes with Rhinestones
Embroidered "Pride of Pageantry" Sweatshirt
Embroidered Garment Bag
Rhinestone Crown Pin

It wasn't Schindler's List, but it was chilling enough. And suddenly I found myself reeling from the thought that I was living in the only society with a uniquely self-canceling insanity: the adults were being driven to make themselves younger while at the same time being driven to make their children older. It was plastic surgery for one and clear plastic shoes for the other: rhinestoned toddlers and face-fixed moms.

Mommy, can I be both the Prettiest Hair and the Most Serious?

Well, Mommy is going for the Most Serious, because I still can't smile, but your whole face can move nicely and I'd like our family to have all the titles, so you go for Smile, Hair, Eyes, Glamour, Cuteness, and Personality.

Mommy, what's personality?

I taught you last night! Don't you remember?

I had thought that preteen pageants were a sickness of only the South, but *Pride of Pageantry* told me that every part of America was now happily devoted to turning small children into large mistakes.

"Welcome! Welcome!" said a young man at a microphone onstage. Smiling even more depressingly than the children, wearing a blue jacket strikingly set against two-toned blond hair, he looked as though he had failed an audition to be a waiter in a topless club. Sensibly, the mothers were ignoring him and creating a buzz of edginess that moved him to say, "Okay now, let's all relax for the competition. I see some of you spitting fire out there and I don't want this to get ugly when our business is *beauty*. . . . All righty, welcome to the talent part of Crystal Dynasty's national talent competition. Let your socks get ready to be knocked off by little queens who've got *all* the Ps: piles of poise, personality, prettiness, and perky packages of pulchritude. And our first talented contestant for our zero to fives is number seventeen, who is almost three, *Brittany!* Welcome, sweetheart!"

To begrudging applause, out came a tot in a pink spangled gown, upswept blond hair, a velvet choker, three strands of pearls, and pink platform shoes. Sashaying across the stage, she made Barbie look like a social worker. Her sensual impact, however, was slightly diminished by the mother kneeling beside her.

Smiling fiercely at the five judges, accompanied by a pianist, Brittany began to sing the world's first erotic rendition of "The Itsy-Bitsy Spider."

Amazing, I thought, remembering Creepy Crawlers. The song works pornographically, too.

To show the falling rain, Brittany wiggled all her fingers, less like a meteorologist than like Gypsy Rose Lee: during the rain, she turned half away from the judges and looked back at them with a beat of lashes that, like her hair, belonged on someone for whom puberty was a memory, not a dream.

When she left the stage after blowing a kiss, I heard her say to her mother, "I did good?"

"You did good," replied the woman who was teaching body, not spoken, English.

"Wonderful, Brittany!" said the MC. "And now let's hear it for number nineteen, three-year-old *Samantha!*"

To more flashing of bulbs and another round of begrudging applause, out came a surrealistic salute to *The Wizard of*

Oz: a tiny girl in a red cocktail dress who looked like one of the Munchkins dressed as Dorothy.

While strobe lights attacked her eyes and her mother coached with exaggerated smiles and gestures from the front row, Samantha sang an a cappella rendition of "Over the Rainbow" in which she was never more than three or four notes from the melody. Her performance would have been better for the Miss New Delhi Pageant because she seemed to be using a twelve-tone scale. At the end of what I think was the song, she threw up both arms as if surrendering and cried, "There's no place like home."

As Samantha left the stage in her ruby slippers, the begrudging applause now seemed to include a strain of the hostile. Walking to her mother, she passed three of her seductive opponents, who were down on the floor near the stage in their gowns, playing with a Game Boy. Even a grotesque enterprise like this pageant couldn't stop kids from being kids, no matter how well disguised as adults they might have been.

Part of the next contestant's disguise was a bouffant hairdo that looked like yellow water wings, which almost matched a two-piece yellow bikini. The two bulges in her bra seemed a touch too much. However, in the zero to five competition, it would have been impossible to detect any one thing that could have been called a touch too much.

As the rock beat of a tape began, the MC said, "Welcome number twelve, three-year-old *Brianna!*" and Brianna began gyrating to "Itsy-Bitsy Teeny-Weeny Yellow Polka Dot Bikini," making the song even more sensual than Brittany's

"The Itsy-Bitsy Spider." What a splendidly all-purpose theme! Would I next be hearing "Itsy-Bitsy Ave Maria"?

Brianna now began singing about her bikini while putting it into a motion that was either adorable or obscene, depending on your appetite for child pornography. While Brianna twisted, her mother gave her whooping encouragement and the other mothers joined in with smiling resentment.

"You *go*, girl!" cried her mother tenderly.

Standing near me, one of the women told another, "Look at *that* one: a designer dress."

"I figured," said the other. "Cut nice in the ass."

"How much you think?"

"Probably twelve hundred."

"I can't go above eight for Lucinda."

"They've got it. This kid won in Louisville."

"The Derby?"

And they both laughed.

As Brianna left the stage to a mixture of whoops and indifferent applause, she hugged herself, and I felt my breakfast rising.

In the following act, a four-year-old named April wore a pink evening gown and had hair that fell to the bottom of her spine.

"Is that her own hair?" I asked a woman beside me.

"It's an *extension*, of course," she said, as if addressing a backward child. "Bad taste. But the velvet choker *is* cool."

"Yes, good taste like the choker is essential," I said while April, also wearing long white gloves, began imitating Marilyn Monroe by slinking around the stage and singing:

A kiss on the hand may be quite continental,
But diamonds are a girl's best friend.

While April was being a pink slinky, her mother coached with passion from just in front of the stage, showing her daughter exaggerated smiles, obligatory turns, and index fingers making dimples in both cheeks. No woman of any age had ever fanned *my* libido by punching at her molars, but these women were experts in the art of seduction, with which they had replaced the art of raising children.

"And now, welcome number twenty-three, who's twenty *less* than that: *Megan!*"

In pink cocktail dress, pink shoes, and blond curls, Megan's Shirley Temple was a poster girl for pedophiles.

"On the good ship *Lollipop*," she screeched, prancing about with her left hand on her hip and swinging her right arm in arcs less fitting for a coquette than a crossing guard. In a remarkable bit of musicianship, she had transposed the entire song to a single note, which happened to be one she couldn't sing. She was, however, able to screw dimples into her cheeks, a feat that was emerging as the major talent of the zero to fives. If one of them *had* possessed a real dimple, her fingers would have been free for cleaning her ears.

"*Sensational*, Megan!" said the MC as the good ship *Lollipop* finished sinking. "And now let's hear it for four-year-old *Alexis!*"

In a sleeveless gown adorned by a dozen pearl clusters, Alexis bounced out, gave herself a hug, and then sang almost to the piano accompaniment:

Button up your overcoat,
When the wind blows free.
Take good care of yourself,
You belong to me!

Throughout her act, most of the enemy mothers kept talking, probably about the bad taste of a four-year-old wearing more than three pearl clusters. Alexis's mother, however, had no time to give these women the finger, because she was preparing to hold up three of them for Alexis to sing, "Get to bed by *three.*" At least the child was learning math.

After Alexis had left the stage, Michelle, who was almost three, burst out in a white cowgirl outfit with a skirt so short that it revealed her Baby Gap panties; and then she began swinging her left arm in circles while her mother mouthed the words of "See What the Boys in the Back Room Will Have," a song that Marlene Dietrich had also performed.

Unfortunately, I was distracted from Michelle's moving salute to Dietrich by a less entertaining scene behind me: a contestant, about three and a half feet tall, was tearfully receiving some last-minute coaching from her mother:

"Roxanne, I don't wanna *hear* it! You're going *up* there!"

"Mommy, I don't *wanna,*" said the star.

"We didn't come all the way from Charlotte for you to just sit there and *cry.* You're goin' for *college* money now!"

After momentarily considering the procurement of her college tuition by shaking her tassled behind, Roxanne replied by pounding her mother with her fists. She clearly belonged on the stage, for she pounded with a nice rhythm. At her feet was a small blue security blanket, but this child needed a security tarpaulin right now.

I probably shouldn't interfere, I thought, *but I think I'll lend the child a hand by killing this woman. The jury not only won't convict me but will give me a Humanitarian of the Year award.*

Here was another parent, like Harry's crazed coach of a father, who should have been required to get a license for parenting after a check on whether or not she happened to be insane. Into my enraged mind now came the memory of a different kind of fight that I had seen near my home just before leaving for Harrisburg. A father and a son about six had been fighting with water guns on their lawn, two duelers gleefully squirting their way to a solid bond.

"The judges will *hear* this," said the mad mother as she dragged her little darling to the back of the room, perhaps to relax her with a general anesthetic, while the MC started to sing "Thank heaven for little girls."

The next morning in the ballroom the Crystal Dynasty Pageant held what it called its Pro-Am event.

"What's Pro-Am?" I asked one of the mothers.

"Oh, it's dancing, acting, sportswear modeling—you name it."

Yes, I could have named it: a scene that made de Sade's basement seem wholesome.

In the zero-to-five division, the pageant now presented the boys in their uniquely tasteless imitations of adults.

"Let's give a sensational welcome," said the MC, "to number seven, five-year-old *Brad*, whose hobbies are watching Rugrats, playing ball, and modeling!"

Out came a small blond boy in white tails, who should have been pinning one on a donkey instead of making a jackass of himself by singing "Making Whoopee" while blowing kisses to adults who didn't want them. Brad's voice was bad, but he also couldn't dance, so his talent was all of a piece; and that piece, the smallest one I had ever seen in formal wear, spent the next three minutes trying to charm five judges, one of whom wore a toupee that came heart-breakingly close to matching his natural hair.

While Brad was busy making me consider suicide, two women near the stage were frantically fussing over the black tuxedo of a small boy who was trying to break free to play with his Game Boy. When Brad left the stage to perfunctory applause, these women launched their creation in that direction.

"And now," said the MC, "let's hear it for *this* sharp-looking young man, number nine, four-year-old *Alex*, whose hobbies are reading and entering pageants and who loves his mother and Mickey Mouse! Alex, go eyeball the judges with that great smile!"

As he began singing "I've Got You Under My Skin," Alex did have a great smile, but the rest of his talent made Brad seem like Baryshnikov. However, his pants-suited mother, so obese that she looked like a polyester *Hindenburg*, thought that Alex was bound for Lincoln Center and gave him the loudest whoops I had heard in the room.

"I've got you deep in the hide of me," sang Alex, although the depths of his hide couldn't hold much. As he pranced about, looking like someone at a black-tie party in Lilliput, he kept taking cues to smile from his massive mother, who was mouthing him toward a thousand-dollar prize.

"And now," said the MC when Brad had shuffled off to the mother ship, "a young gentleman of three, *Armando*, whose hobbies are entering pageants, playing in the dirt, and visiting patients at a VA nursing home!"

Swinging a black cane, Armando came strutting out to start singing "Strangers in the Night."

"Dooby-dooby-do," he sang, words he might have been speaking just a couple of years ago. From time to time, he waved his cane awkwardly and flashed a frightened smile at the judges. Standing in the front row of the audience, his mother kept sticking out her tongue at him. At first I thought she was giving him a review, but then I realized that she was trying to loosen him up. However, he still seemed more nervous than he probably was in the dirt or the nursing home. He could have used a formal pacifier.

Halfway through his act, Armando took off his dinner jacket and tossed it from the stage, trying to look like Sinatra. At last, after he had doobied his last doo, he strutted off to his mother, who now used her tongue to say, "You did *good*, baby!"

"Can I play, Mommy?" the young swinger replied.

"Win this pageant, baby, and we'll *both* play."

"I wanna play *now*."

"Armie, you gotta stay sharp for the sportswear modeling. Gettin' messed up by play is the *last* thing . . . anyway, what's to play in this place?"

"They got Barbies."

"*Who* got 'em?" said the mother in alarm.

Armando pointed to two small queens on the floor who were playing with Barbies. One of them wore a black leather miniskirt and the other a feathered boa around her neck. The Barbies could have played with *them*.

"Them," said Armando.

"Christ, they're *girls!* That's all we *need:* for the judges to catch you cross-playin'!"

For the next half hour, as the intense competition continued, it seemed to me that hips were twisting faster and buttocks were bobbing harder and lashes were batting more fiercely than I had seen in the earlier acts. Of course, I might have been wrong because I was trying to forget the earlier acts. I also was trying to forget a scene I had stumbled upon a few hours ago in a corner of the hotel lounge: two small children with rollers in their hair and two mothers with steel in their hearts. The mothers were talking to each other as if the children weren't there, just as all the other mothers were acting as if the pageant had no children.

"Where you guys goin' next?" said one circuit rider to another.

"Mount Holly," said the other, "if we don't run out of money."

"Mount Holly? That Arkansas?"

"New Jersey."

"Well, it's all the same. Still gotta sleep in curlers and smile the shit outa the judges."

"Money. That Samantha—you know, the one with the ass like a hippo—said she's spent twenty thousand in the last three years and she's won only eight. She's fifteen down."

"But it's still worth it for the kids."

"Damn right. You think I'm doin' this for *myself?* It's one terrific lesson for the kids in how to succeed. If you don't win this one, you go on to the next and try a little harder. Arianna is gonna get beat a lot and she needs to learn how to lose. They sure don't get that in school." At last noting the presence of her daughter, she said, "Okay, Arianna, lemme hear it again."

"I need the music," said the child.

"No, this is gonna be al cappella, so lemme hear it an' stop talkin' back."

Grimly, the child began to sing:

> *Whe-e-e-e-ere is love?*
> *Whe-e-e-e-ere is love?*

Long after the last contestant had slunk off the stage, that question was sounding in my brain.

16

All You Need
Is Love

For many days after the pageant, I was haunted by having
been to the black pit of push-parenting. The Bright Start
Learning Center suddenly seemed like a sleepy sandbox,
Harry's father like Sportsman of the Year, and Glenn
Doman like Mr. Chips. And then I came across a book
called *Baby Minds: Brain-Building Games Your Baby Will
Love* and I remembered that the mishandling of children in
America has an infinite variety.

Written by two San Francisco psychologists named
Linda Acredolo and Susan Goodwyn, the book has several
itsy-bitsy new insights into remaking babies, such as:

*Just because your three-month-old can't answer questions
about the past doesn't mean you shouldn't bring the subject up
for discussion.*

Birth to six months: Talk to your baby about ongoing events.

*By the time your child is eighteen months old, you can expect
him to begin Dialogic Reading in earnest.*

The mind doesn't reel, it flies into orbit. All my talks with first-rate pediatricians, first-rate psychologists, and a first-rate wife have told me that such ideas belong at barber college, although they lack the intellectual depth of how to shampoo.

I am, of course, distressed that many three-month-old children, like older ones, no longer care about history; many times I tried to make my own children start studying it. When Lori was three months old and still undecided about her major, I asked her if she thought that Truman was still underrated. Alas, she just didn't give a damn.

Moreover, whatever dialogic reading Lori may have done for her first three years was never in earnest. From the beginning, she giggled her way through each airy page of *Goodnight Moon,* although *my* part was delivered in the style of the Old Vic. She did seem a bit more serious during *Go Dog Go!,* but in that one, *I* was never able to repress a certain giddiness.

Linda Acredolo, Susan Goodwyn, Glenn Doman, Crawling Alice, Belted Janet, Gettysburg Sam, and the millions of parents who have redefined baby boomer all have endlessly focused on flash cards while being blind to the great timeless truth that I learned in the depths of push-parenting: It is madness to try to force babies to read. Instead, let them explore their world. Let them crawl around it, pick things up, and make more important connections than the name of the head of admissions at Yale.

"When babies crawl, they learn from their environment," says Barbara L. Kornblau, president of the American

Occupational Therapy Association, echoing Professors Elkind and Ruddy. "It's exploration needed for brain development."

The Better Baby people need to work on their *own* brain development, for they have it backward: They feel that very early reading makes children more precocious, but the route is the *other* way: precocious children tend to be early readers. However, let us remember that early reading has no effect on the IQ and no bearing on whether a child will end up in the Institute for Advanced Studies or the Witness Protection Program.

Because raising children who will avoid the Witness Protection Program is always a blend of groping, hoping, love, and luck, because parenting is an endeavor as scientific as communication with the Tooth Fairy, there are no absolute rules for it, or even relative ones—except perhaps: Less can be more. The enlightened way to raise children is not by pushing but by using a lower gear, and sometimes neutral.

Two of my neighbors are a husband and wife, both about forty. Almost every snowless day one of them plays baseball or basketball outside their house with two sons who are eight and ten. These adults play with such happy ease that it seems to me unlikely that the boys will ever honor the spirit of Harry's father by enlivening games with elbows and knees inserted into opposing kidneys and groins.

One twilight in June, after one of the boys had made a head fake against his defender and then driven in for a layup, I said, "Molly, you're a lousy point guard but a wonderful mother."

"I'm just keeping an eye on them," she replied, "until they're legal adults."

These words should be burned into the cluttered calendars of every parent who has entered a child in a marathon leading to a finish that might be the finish of the child. They are words that should move every fast tracker to stop playing academic dominoes and start enjoying the roll of the dice that raising children forever will be.

Even if the entire fad of push-parenting gives way to one of equal sense, like hang gliding over Niagara Falls, parenting will never again be what it was when Judy and I were raising not résumés but kids. Like Molly, we allowed all three of ours to grow up without acceleration; and all three are now happy, intelligent, and creative adults, in spite of having done only unstructured crawling, of having learned to read post–crawling, and of having heard only the soft lapping of amniotic fluid in the womb.

Because our youngest, Lori, had shown no interest in history at three months, she lacked the foundation for any discussion of ongoing events at six months, and she was further handicapped by knowing no words. It was not until she was three years old, alarmingly behind the Bay Area babes, that I finally gave her an introduction to the richness of the English language.

We were down on the living room floor, playing with magnetic letters and shapes. Lori was making a fence to protect an imaginary garden, while I had almost finished spelling a thoughtful reflection on the state of the economy: SCREW IT ALL. As I was taking a piece for my final *l*, Lori grabbed it.

"I need this," she said, and she put it on her fence.

"No, honey," I said, gently taking back the piece, "it's the last straight one and *Daddy* needs it to finish his word. I don't want to say, 'SCREW IT AL,' because I don't *know* any Al. So make your fence shorter."

"Fence to stop animals in garden," she said to a man who saw no need to rush her out of speaking like Sitting Bull.

"Plant pachysandra instead," I said.

A few minutes later she came to my desk for one of her frequent visits, climbed into my lap, and began to collaborate with me by pressing my typewriter keys.

"Daddy is trying to work now," I told her, "and it's probably better if he hits all the keys by himself. He knows where all of them are."

"I stay here and help you with homework," she said, putting her cheek against mine.

And once again I thought, *This is as good as it gets.* What I did not think of was teaching her the Latin for love.

Acknowledgement:

Lines from *Diamonds Are a Girl's Best Friend* by Jule Styne and Leo Robin, used by permissiion of Music Sales Corporation.

Author photo; credit: Judith Schoenstein

A nationally acclaimed writer and broadcaster who has been widely syndicated and anthologized, Ralph Schoenstein is the author of sixteen books, including *The Block, Citizen Paul,* and the best-selling *The I-Hate-Preppies Handbook.* Holder of the Playboy Award for Humor, he writes for *Newsday,* the *Daily News,* and the *New York Times* and is a commentator for NPR's "All Things Considered." He lives in Princeton, New Jersey, where he enjoys having no connection to the university and he has three grandchildren, all world class.